SEEKING GOD
WHILE SERVING TIME

To Elizabeth,
May you be inspired
by these stories — as I have —
Keep up your great spirit

Peace
Mark McKenna

SEEKING GOD
WHILE SERVING TIME

The Faith Journey of Women in Jail

"An inspirational book of how God blesses in difficult times and a tremendous resource on how we and our churches can help women in prison."
CHARLES COLSON
AUTHOR OF *BORN AGAIN* AND *LIFE SENTENCE*

Gail Thomas McKenna

Pleasant Word
A Division of WINEPRESS PUBLISHING

Pleasant Word (a division of WinePress Publishing, PO Box 428, Enumclaw, WA 98022) functions only as book publisher. As such, the ultimate design, content, editorial accuracy, and views expressed or implied in this work are those of the author.

Unless otherwise noted, all Scriptures are taken from the *New American Standard Bible,* © 1960, 1963, 1968, 1971, 1972, 1973, 1975, 1977 by The Lockman Foundation. Used by permission.

ISBN 13: 978-1-4141-1164-3
ISBN 10: 1-4141-1164-9
Library of Congress Catalog Card Number: 2007910286

Dedicated to the memory of the late
Gina Immormino
I wanted her to coauthor this book, but
God took her to His side before she could begin ...

... and to my lifelong friend,
Sister Agnes Arvin, S.P.
for her love, guidance, and support.

CONTENTS

INTRODUCTION

"What is it like being inside a jail?"
"How did you get involved in this ministry?"
"Do you find the women you meet want to change their lives?"
"What do you do when you meet with the women each week?"

THESE ARE BUT a few of the many questions I have been asked since I began my ministry with the women in our county jail. For most people, knowledge of what happens in their local jail is limited to what they read in the papers, or see on their local television each night. When they encounter someone who actually goes inside, they have their first opportunity to find out the real story. And so the questions begin.

As I began answering these questions, I realized that many people are interested in learning about what happens to those who are arrested and sent to jail. Since I had previously written about my twenty-five-year parish ministry as a Director of Religious Education, it seemed only fitting that I should do the same for my new work as a volunteer in our county jail. I realize there are many who have dedicated more years to this field than I have, and who could no doubt present a more comprehensive picture. But I have been blessed with the luxury of time at this stage of my life, and a love for writing, and so I felt called to write this book—a book not only of my experiences over the past ten years, but more importantly, the stories of the women with whom I have come in contact in this ministry. Their stories motivated me to write: stories of pain, suffering, loneliness, intimidation, and rejection, but also stories of faith and hope.

I have changed the names of the inmates to safeguard their identities, but I have not changed their stories. They are all true. When I heard of experiences worth passing on, I found myself jotting down notes so I wouldn't forget them. I mentioned to the women my plans to share their stories in a book, and they were both supportive and interested. At the same time, they gave me permission to do so. I am grateful to them for allowing me to do this.

Over the past years, the one theme that kept recurring was how the experience of being in jail has helped so many women reconnect to God. If I've heard it once, I've heard it a hundred times: words like, "The best thing that happened to me was being put here. I finally have been able to stop and think and get my priorities in order. I now have time for God and reading His Word. This has changed my life." This recurring message inspired me to title this book *Seeking God While Serving Time.*

I will begin with the story of how I became involved in this ministry. After this, I will walk you through one of our weekly sessions—time where we share our lives, search the Scriptures, sing, and pray together.

In the following chapters, I'll go beyond that hour to the daily lives of the women, what they do, what they possess, and where they find ways to include God. The special times to bring God into their lives come through celebrations of the church's year: Ash Wednesday, Lent, Advent and Christmas. They also occur during the retreat weekends scheduled twice each year—a real high point for both the inmates and the retreat team.

Along with the sessions I am involved in, there are other opportunities for the women to deepen their faith life and experience the support of community. In order to include these, I attended some of these gatherings and talked to other group leaders. I also asked different women to share their reactions. This gave me many other experiences to pass on to you.

These programs provide those first steps for change, but it is only a beginning. Our hope is that it will lead to a better life. Unfortunately, it is a well known fact that jails seem to have a revolving door with many repeat offenders, and I've seen that to be true. However, we can't lose hope. It's through programs like these, offered to help the women truly change, that they can begin to change.

Where they go from here is the challenge facing not only those in jail ministry, but more importantly, the whole of society. We will look at the ways that we in society, and especially in the church, can continue to nourish the women seeking our help.

And finally, I challenge you to make some commitment to this cause. Maybe you're not ready to "get on the bus" and meet the people. But that doesn't mean you should shut the door on this message of Christ to visit the imprisoned. My own life has been rewarded countless times since I answered that call. Those same blessings await you.

Yes, there is still much that is wrong with our jails and prisons. I don't pretend to be a reformer. But I do know this: if I can help one person within those walls feel she is important and loved, that God cares about her, and so do we ... that is enough.

My gratitude goes out to all who have invited and encouraged me in this ministry—especially to the dedicated staff of chaplains at the women's annex: Sister Teresa Carter, CSB, Reverend Carl Schindler, CSSR, Deacon Gilbert Pratt and Sister Ellen McRedmond, DC. I am also indebted to the priests, Reverend Father Enda McKenna and Kevin Ryan, who celebrate the monthly liturgy with us as well as my two co-leaders, Anita Benton and Bea Asfeld, who join me each week for prayer and reflections with the women inmates. And as I mentioned earlier, my gratitude extends to the hundreds of women who have enriched my life by sharing their stories, their personal journeys of faith. Finally, I want to thank my dear husband, Jerry, who encouraged me to write this book and patiently edited every page of the manuscript before going to press.

May these stories be a source of inspiration to you, as they have been to me.

Chapter 1

THE GOD OF SURPRISES

THE LONGER I live, the more I realize that life is full of surprises. Becoming involved in jail ministry was truly one of those surprises. I might add we should never say never to situations in life. It was almost thirty years ago that I muttered that word **never**, only to find I was wrong.

Back in 1978, I was working as Director of Religious Education in Nebraska. We were living in Papillion at the time and, because of my work in another parish, I was seldom able to attend the local church a few miles from our home. This particular Sunday, however, was a family Sunday, which meant no religion classes for the children and no work for me. And so I was able to join my family for Mass at our local church, St. Columbkille.

During that homily, we were challenged to take to heart the gospel message of visiting the imprisoned. The priest was even going to make it easy for us. He had hired a bus. All we needed to do was gather in the parish parking lot at 2:00 P.M., and we'd go as a group to the nearby prison. I listened to his words, a little uncomfortable with his request. My immediate response was, "Not me. That's not my calling. I could never do that. Besides, I'm already doing the Lord's work, directing the religion programs for all the children, teens, and adults in the parish in which I was working.

Isn't that enough? And this is my Sunday off." Needless to say, I wasn't on the bus that afternoon.

Fast forward to 1998. I had just completed twenty-five years as a Director of Religious Education (DRE). I was ready to officially step out of full-time ministry and move into the next phase of my life. My elderly parents, both in their nineties, were coming to live with my husband and me in our comfortable hill-country home in Texas. And our five children were now grown and out on their own. I was entering a new phase of my life, ready to get serious about my writing again, with the luxury of time and new experiences to share.

And then God opened a new door to me. Although I was serious about my writing and sensitive to the needs of my parents, I felt something was missing in my life. I needed more people to interact with during the course of the day. Over the past twenty-some years, my life had been surrounded with people. Along with the challenges and joys of raising five children and maintaining a loving relationship with my husband, I had been a full-time DRE. There were people everywhere. Now, retired from my job and with my children gone, I felt a vacuum, a void that didn't go unnoticed by my dear friend, Sister Teresa.

Sister was the chaplain of our local county jail. She was busy organizing a group to present a retreat for the women at the jail, which was being held the next weekend. We were visiting over a cup of tea when she casually told me about the retreat, and invited me to drop in and meet the women while getting a peek at what was going on. She knew I was no longer employed at parish work and would be able to come. I think she also knew I was searching for some type of ministry to get involved in. Whatever the reason, she hit a nerve and I felt drawn to accept her invitation.

My intention was just to stop by that Saturday afternoon, maybe spend an hour with the ladies. After years in parish work organizing retreats, I thought it would be interesting to see the difference in this retreat. And so I went to the jail.

I vividly remember that first encounter with the women inmates. There were about thirty of them making this retreat, led by a group of fifteen volunteers from one of the local parishes. The atmosphere was alive and buzzing. Women were deeply engrossed in conversations, some sobbing, others laughing, everyone involved in the discussion at hand. I was immediately drawn into a conversation with seven women gathered around a small table. These ladies opened my eyes to a new world, a world I had only read about in the papers, or heard about on the local nightly news. They were so honest in their sharing, so fragile and hurt from life's experiences. For once, I was the listener, not the talker. The elderly woman next to me told me she was going to be released in two weeks. She had been active in her local church, and was eager to get back to her friends there. I was impressed by her sincerity, and promised to remember her in my prayers.

I stayed that afternoon and watched how the women became so involved with the volunteers. They would stand and pray for each of the presenters before they began their talk. They would respond in song and testimonies.

I remained with the group until the final prayer that day. And I returned the next morning for the closing exercises. I was hooked.

Immediately I sought out Sister Teresa and asked to be included as a member of the next retreat team. One thing led to another and, after that second retreat weekend, I was ready to become a regular member of the volunteer community for the county jail. After these retreat experiences, someone needed to help the women continue their walk with the Lord. I wanted to be that someone. I had found what was missing from my life—people I could minister to on a weekly basis. And I eagerly waited to see how this work would unfold for me in the upcoming months.

Before I actually began to minister, I prayed for wisdom and guidance. This was a whole new world for me, and I wasn't sure I could tackle it alone. I've always believed there was a reason Jesus sent out his disciples two by two. In fact, when I directed parish programs, I followed His example and always assigned two teachers to every classroom or two adults to each youth group. I was now the disciple, so my next task was to look for a companion to join me in my new ministry.

Inmates praying for the speaker

I remembered a friend who had worked with me in the parish, who had voiced her desire to become involved in some type of caring ministry. She was presently unemployed and, due to health reasons, only available for a few hours each week. Why not ask her if she'd like to join me in this weekly session at the jail? To my delight, Anita accepted my invitation, and the following week, the two of us were in the offices of the county jail being fingerprinted, photographed for I.D. badges, and given TB tests. Within days, and with a little trepidation, we reported in to meet our first class. There were about twelve women awaiting our presence. And so we began to share the *good news*—we began to walk with them on their faith journey.

That was ten years ago. And today, after several retreats and ongoing weekly sessions throughout the year with incarcerated women, I am ready to share some of their stories. These stories have changed my life and have deepened my own faith, because they have shown me the power of God: stories of how God touches us in all circumstances of our lives, and stories of how His grace causes change in our lives, especially in the lives of women who have taken a wrong turn, or been involved with people who have made bad choices, or become slaves of drugs, alcohol, or greed.

Yes, God is a God of surprises. And I thank Him every day for the opportunity to walk with these women, making them a part of my life, of my journey of faith. As the years have gone by, the stories of the women have given me many surprises. Now it's time to let you in on the good news.

Chapter 2

THE GOOD NEWS ... AND NOT-SO-GOOD NEWS

I T'S AROUND NOON on Monday—that means it's time to leave for the county jail. There will be anywhere from fifteen to thirty women awaiting my arrival at exactly 2:00 P.M. My new co-leader, Bea, usually manages to arrive before I do to greet the ladies and welcome them. Bea had asked to become part of our team since Anita's health frequently kept her from participating. You can never have too many volunteers.

The inmates are escorted to our room—the chapel—although it is basically just a room set with chairs in rows facing a table. The table is actually an altar that was donated by the Sisters in a local convent. Some of the women will be familiar faces, women who have been there for weeks or months awaiting a trial date. Others will be new to the group. Some are encouraged by their friends to come, and others sign up anxious to share their faith, while a few just pop in out of curiosity. All are welcome. Since no one is forced to attend any of the church services or classes, we usually don't have to deal with disruptive behavior.

The women come from different units called pods (place of domicile). These are dormitory-type rooms, housing at least fifty women in each. This is basically their home while they are awaiting trial, either to be sentenced to a state prison or released from the jail. It's not the most comfortable of situations, with bunk beds aligned closely together, limited bathing facilities, and little space for anything private. But then, this is jail, not a hotel.

Coming together each week does provide the women with a brief escape from this environment, and helps them cope with the harshness of everyday life.

And so either Bea or I begin each session focusing on the positive—the good news in their life today, their gospel for this week. You would think this group of women would be the last to have something good to share with others. These women are confined to tight quarters with no freedom to move about, surrounded by numerous other women with no space except a bunk bed to call their own, and yet never a week passes that we don't hear a few stories of good news and hope. In fact, the more the group begins to form a community, the more open they are to sharing something positive in their life.

Becky begins with her story. "I finally got a letter from my teenage son. He's not happy I'm here, but at least we are communicating again. He still isn't comfortable coming here to visit me, but says he'll continue to write me now. And I'm going to answer his letters so we can mend some bridges."

Shanna is anxious to add her good news, because she saw her grandchild for the first time last Saturday. She has heard me share stories about my grandchildren, and it made her anxious to hold her own grandson. When she called her daughter and begged her to come and bring the new baby, she was delighted by how open her daughter was to the idea. Now her daughter promises to continue to visit with the baby more often, so Shanna won't miss out completely on her first years. After Shanna told of her experience, a few of the women were in tears, and they all clapped. It was truly a sign of love and support for this grandmother.

Next, Jeanette wants us to know she is going to trial on Tuesday morning. All her papers are ready, and she is hoping she will be released on probation. We promise our remembrance of her in our prayers for that morning. I make a note of this so I, too, will remember her in my morning prayer time on Tuesday when I gather with my faith community.

THE GOOD NEWS … AND NOT-SO-GOOD NEWS

I am about to move into the next segment when I notice Pat raising her hand. She's hidden behind a taller woman in the back of the room. Pat says, "I'm from California and have served there more than once because of my involvement with drugs. A few weeks ago, I was picked up here in Texas. That's why I am here. I need to tell you it's the first time I found God in all these years, in all these sentences. So I want to proudly state before you all my good news is I found God in Texas. And now my life will never be the same. I thank God I came here…to serve time for my crimes, but more importantly, to get my life back on track."

Everyone applauds Pat's good news. I think some realize they are part of her conversion.

Of course, not everyone has good news to announce each week. But just hearing from a few of the ladies sets the tone for our gathering. In the midst of all the negativism around them, there is something positive to focus on, if only for a few minutes. Bea and I sometimes add a personal note about our situations, especially something they can relate to and look forward to when they are free, such as a family birthday or celebration.

One day, one of the women approached me after our session and thanked me for sharing my personal life with them. "You make us feel part of your family," she said. "When you talk about your ninety-six year old father, I feel like I know him. And I look forward to what tidbit you'll share with us next week. I wish you could bring him here, but I know that's impossible." This makes me feel the closeness of our group.

I remember when my dear mother was dying a few years ago. It was this jail community who became my support and encouragement during those last months. It was then that I realized this ministry was a two-way deal. We were all benefiting from each other by our time together.

Before we move into the next part of our session, it's important to have time to talk about the "not-so-good news" of the past week, sharing those situations over the past days where we turn to God for the help we need, and the support of this community to make it through. There are always some ready to add their story, asking for our prayers.

Donna begins, "My mom went to the doctor for tests this past week because she was feeling very worn out. It turns out she has cancer, and she's so afraid. She lives by herself, and I was the only one who ever gave her any help. Now, look where I'm at when she really needs me. I feel so bad. Please pray for her … and me. I wish I were out of here so I could help her again." And then she sobs while others go to comfort her.

Rosalinda tells us she had just heard from her mother who is taking care of her teenage son. He is causing her some problems. She tells her he is staying out too late at night and is getting out of control. Rosalinda says, "I feel so terrible that I am here when he needs me. I can't expect my mother, who is not in good health, to put up with him. I'm afraid he's going to end up across the street in the men's unit, because I know those friends he hangs around with are up to no good."

It must be so hard for Rosalinda and other mothers to be cut off from their children at such crucial times in their lives. Many of the mothers have given their children to their parents to raise while they are incarcerated. And sometimes their spouses or siblings are responsible for them. At least these children are being kept within the family, and are still connected to their parent through visiting times. But there are many cases where the children have been placed in foster homes temporarily, and this is definitely harder on the mothers serving time.

Lastly, Johanna asks us all to pray for her. She went to court last week and found out she would have to serve eighteen more months at the state prison. She was hoping they would give her probation and she'd be reunited with her family. Her only hope now is money to pay her bail—money she just doesn't have. Money is a real problem for so many of the women who are incarcerated. They can't come up with the bail, so they are forced to remain in jail while they are waiting for their court date.

Not all of the women are comfortable telling their stories of need. These are stories too painful to share in public, or too sensitive for all to know about. Before we close our meeting each week, we take these intentions and place them with others' needs as we make our circle of prayer.

THE GOOD NEWS ... AND NOT-SO-GOOD NEWS

We create our circle of prayer as the women leave their chairs and join hands, forming a large circle. Sometimes it's just a small circle of fifteen women, but most of the time it encompasses the whole room, as twenty-five to thirty inmates join hands. During this prayerful moment, each woman has an opportunity to include her special intentions as we move from left to right around the circle. There are numerous requests for families, spouses, boyfriends, children, other inmates, and court dates placed before the Lord at this time. If anyone is uncomfortable voicing their petition, or feel their needs have already been prayed for, they squeeze the hand of the person next to them and the prayer circle continues. Bea and I also include our intentions with those of the inmates. Once the circle is complete, we lift up all our petitions to the Lord and raise our joined hands as we say the prayer that Jesus taught us: "The Lord's Prayer."

This is the end of our class. Before we recite this closing prayer, we have over an hour to listen to the good news of Scripture, share it with others, and make it come alive within these walls.

Chapter 3

THE GOSPEL COMES ALIVE

THERE IS ONE item everyone who enters the jail is entitled to: a Bible. And for most, this becomes a treasure they cherish. In order to receive a Bible, they must first submit a request form—a green slip. Since almost all of the Bibles are donated to the jail, there are a variety of translations. In most instances, the women don't care whether it's a King James Version, a New American Bible, or an annotated version. In fact, they usually ask for a specific Bible by describing the cover. Those with modern scenes or large print are more popular. The rule is that they may only have one Bible; therefore, it's recorded when it is given to them. But even with this system, there are slip-ups discovered when belongings are inventoried before leaving the jail. Mysteriously, two Bibles will tumble out of the pillowcase, one with a lovely scene, the other with a plain cover. At least this shows the Holy Book has taken on some importance in their lives.

For many of these women, it's the first time they actually have time to open and read the Scriptures. On more than one occasion, they have asked me to help them understand how to find particular passages. Periodically, we will spend six weeks covering the basics of Scripture. For some, it opens up a whole new world. Having left behind their addictions to drugs, alcohol, and worldly luxuries,

Bea giving an inmate a Bible

they can turn their energies toward loftier ideals. And many do just that, as they take time to listen to God speaking to them through Scripture. They have told me how consoling it is to read their Bible before the lights are dimmed for sleep. Their bunk bed actually becomes the sacred space where they can meditate and pray undisturbed. It's the one place they can seek refuge from the chaos around them.

In some pods, they will gather around the table in small groups during the day to read the Scriptures and pray together. Those who are more familiar and comfortable with the meaning of the Bible usually take on a leadership role in this group. None of this is mandated or scripted by those in charge. It is truly the Spirit at work, drawing two or three together. And it becomes a source of nourishment and support for the women who take advantage of this opportunity.

In our weekly gathering, we focus on the Scripture readings from Sunday's liturgy. It is the heart of our gathering time. After telling of their good and not-so-good news, we move into the readings from Scripture for the week. To set the mood, I like to play an applicable religious song or some soft music. This is followed with an opening prayer based on the theme from our readings for the day.

When I first began this ministry, it took some time to feel comfortable as a leader of the group. Even though I had years of experience directing small discussion groups, this group was different. We had no history together. I didn't know their background, nor did they know mine. But I knew it was important to establish a good rapport with them. I decided to begin with a question about them, before we moved into any Scripture. I wanted to know what brought them to this Christian class. So I asked the simple question, "Why are you here?"

I was taken aback when Maria responded without hesitation, "I was involved in a gang, peddling drugs and …" Before she went any further, I interrupted her to clarify my question. "Maria," I said, "I didn't mean to ask why you are here in the county jail; I meant why you are here in this room today. Why did you come to our class?"

The entire class was amused, and probably relieved that I didn't care to know why they were serving time. That was not my intent. I came to minister to them and was only interested in walking with them on their faith journey.

After hearing from a few of the inmates, we opened the Bible. The Word was proclaimed, pondered, and finally shared by the women. When our numbers are too large for everyone to give their input aloud, we break into groups of two or three for the initial sharing. This allows time for both introverts and extroverts to be more at ease expressing themselves. After a few minutes of sharing in small groups, we come together as a large unit. Before adding our input as leaders, we carefully listen to their reactions to the readings. We remind them there are no right and wrong answers. The Spirit works in each of us. All are welcome to share their thoughts and feelings with the larger group. The goal is to encourage them to put flesh on the words written and spoken over 2000 years ago, to make the gospel come alive!

The women have told us endless stories over the years of how the readings from Scripture apply to their life. It would take another book to relay them all to you. However, by focusing in on three stories in Scripture that have touched their lives, we will see how meaningful the Word is to them.

We will begin with the parable of the lost son—the prodigal son, as told to us in the gospel of Luke 15:11-25.

> A man had two sons and the younger son said to his father, "Father, give me your share of the estate that should come to me." So the father divided the property between them. After a few days, the younger son collected all his belongings and set out to a distant country where he squandered his inheritance on a life of dissipation. When he had freely spent everything a severe famine struck the country and he found himself in dire need. So he hired himself out to one of the local citizens who sent him to his farm to tend the swine. And he longed to eat his fill on the husks on which the swine fed, but nobody gave him any. Coming to his senses, he thought 'How many of my father's workers have more than enough to eat, but here I am dying of hunger. I shall get up and go to my father and I shall say to him, "Father, I have sinned against heaven and against you. I no longer deserve to be called your son, treat me as you would treat your hired workers."' So he got up and went back to his father. While he was still a long way off, his father caught sight of him and was filled with compassion. He ran to his son and embraced him and kissed him. His son said to him, "Father, I have sinned against heaven and against you. I no longer deserve to be called your son." But his father ordered his servants, "Quickly bring out the finest robe and put it on him; put a ring on his fingers and sandals on his feet. Take the fattened calf and slaughter it. Then let us celebrate with a feast, because this son of mine was dead and has come to life again; he was lost and has been found."

The story continues with the elder brother returning to hear the celebration taking place, and becoming angry because he feels his own faithfulness has never been rewarded. And his father reminds him that everything he has is his, but now we must celebrate his brother's return.

What a powerful story Jesus tells us. And what a message it has for these women gathered in prayer. Rita begins with her personal application of this parable. She says:

> "I felt like the prodigal daughter returning home, except instead of getting a party and celebration, I'm treated like the black sheep. I know this because this is my second time in jail and I've had one homecoming. It wasn't a happy one. And I'm not looking forward to the next, because everything is the same, my parents and siblings are embarrassed, my friends ignore me, and the neighbors all seem to be whispering as I walk down the street. I just wish someone would greet me with a smile and welcome me back like the father in this story."

What a sad commentary on the labels we place on someone incarcerated. No wonder so many return to the scene of their crimes. It may be the only place they feel welcome. After Rita's comments, others offer her words of encouragement by telling her how they overcame some of those same feelings. They tell her about support groups and church organizations where she can go and feel good about herself, instead of ashamed. She was grateful for their advice, and promised to take advantage of some of these opportunities when she is released in a few months.

Another woman adds her thoughts on this same gospel:

> "I, too, can relate to the prodigal son. I left my home because of drugs. It was a quick way to make money and give me all those things I was deprived of living in the ghetto. Before I knew it, I had a new fancy car, nice designer clothes, and lots of cash. I liked that. And then I got caught and it was all over. Everything was taken away from me, and here I am serving time for my foolishness. I've really had time to think since I came here. I know I'll be sent to the state prison, but I also know all the stuff wasn't worth it. Some of my new friends here in jail have shown me how to be happy. We pray together every night, and read the Bible, and I feel better. I'll admit I was foolish like that son, but I know that God, like the father, still loves me, and I'm going to try to change my ways, return to a better life, and follow Him."

I believe this gospel is one of the most poignant ones for anyone who has gone astray. It is a sign of encouragement if we focus on the role of the father, who is waiting—always waiting—to embrace the person who has left home. And this story has a happy ending.

Before concluding this gathering, Sherry asked if she could add her comments on this story. She begins:

> "I really goofed. I was on the fast track … drugs, alcohol, the night life. Boy, could I party! I was what you called 'hot' and it was great! But you know what I'm going to say next, right? It didn't last. Before I knew it, my boyfriend and I had nowhere to go. Our parents didn't want us around. Our so-called 'friends' weren't there when we needed a place to hang out. When you've suddenly got no place to hide, you become very visible and can't escape the law. It happened … and here I sit. My boyfriend is across the street at the men's jail. I've heard this story from the Bible before, but now it's finally beginning to make sense. I need to come to my senses. I hope I can make it."

These testimonies make the words of Scripture relevant for all of us in the twenty-first century. And there are numerous other passages in Scripture that revolve around the same theme of understanding the wrongdoing, seeking forgiveness, and realizing there is a loving Father always ready to forgive.

The second gospel story we will look at is the parable of the sower and the seed scattered along the ground. In St. Matthew's gospel, we read:

> On that day, Jesus went out of the house and sat down by the sea. Such large crowds gathered around him that he got into a boat and sat down, and the whole crowd stood along the shore. And he spoke to them at length in parables, saying:

> A sower went out to sow. And as he sowed, some seed fell on the path, and birds came and ate it up. Some fell on rocky ground, where it had little soil. It sprang up at once because the soil was not deep, and when the sun rose it was scorched, and it withered for lack of roots. Some seed fell among thorns, and the thorns grew up and choked it. But some seed fell on rich soil,

and produced fruit, a hundred or sixty or thirty fold. Whoever has ears ought to hear."

—Matthew 13:1-10

After listening to these words, we spent a few moments in silence pondering how they touched our lives today. I asked the women to think about how they could become the seed planted in the rich soil in God's eyes, so they too could produce good things. The women shared these ideas:

Laurie began, "Love is like a flower that needs good soil, sun, and rain to grow. Only in that rich soil will it grow and shine before others. I know that all that pleasure I was seeking caused just lots of pain—no love, no growth. But then I found a friend in Jesus. He will always be around to help me grow and He will never let me down."

Chris added, "Now I am fertilizing my soul to make it rich by reading the Word to gain insight into who Jesus was and is for me. I ask Him for wisdom, knowledge, and understanding in order to be fruitful for others. I have complete peace and I am content being here. Being unselfish and giving to others is a main fruit I hope to bear."

Others shared their thoughts on this reading, mentioning how both drugs and alcohol can choke the soul and drive God out, and how keeping company with the wrong people makes their lives shallow. This is one of the biggest temptations they have to resist when they return to the free world. So often they end up back in jail because of these so-called friends who attract them back to the drug scene.

The third and final passage I would like to mention is that of Zaccheus, the tax collector Jesus called down from the tree and invited to dine with him. We read:

He came to Jericho and intended to pass through the town. Now a man there named Zaccheus, who was a chief tax collector and also a wealthy man, was seeking to see who Jesus was; but he could not see him because of the crowd, for he was short in stature. So he ran ahead and climbed a sycamore tree in order to see Jesus, who was about to pass that way. When he reached the place Jesus looked up and said, " Zaccheus, come down quickly, for today I must stay at your house." And he came down quickly and received him with joy. When they all saw this they began to grumble saying, "He has gone to stay at the house of a sinner." But Zaccheus stood there and said to the Lord, "Behold, half of my possessions, Lord, I shall give to the poor, and if I have extorted anything from anyone I shall repay it four times over." And Jesus said to him, "Today salvation has come to this house because this man is a descendant of Abraham. For the Son of Man has come to seek and save what is lost."

—Luke 19:1-10

This last sentence of the story has a message that strikes home for the women. After hearing of Zaccheus, it was time to talk about how we can relate to him and his situation when we too have felt loss and want to seek Jesus in our lives.

Tearfully Linda tells us how she is so lost without her two children who are two and eight years old. They are now in the care of their godparents, and she thinks they are trying to separate them from her permanently. She tells us that, on a recent visit home before she was incarcerated, her young son noticed her across the street and yelled, "Mommy," only to be taken inside by the godmother. She's so afraid he will forget her. And she feels so alone, being separated from these children. The other women encourage her to keep this memory alive in her heart, and when they are reunited everything will be all right. Since many of them are separated from their loved ones, they can be empathetic with Linda.

Yvonne shared her feelings of being lost—lost in the world of drugs. She said, "When you're on the street and shooting up, you lose all touch with reality. You may feel high for awhile, but then you feel miserable … truly lost and alone. There's no one who really cares about you when you're in that state. It's every person for herself. And forget about your family. They want no part of you or your lifestyle. It's not worth it."

Charlene told us how she felt Jesus came to seek her when she was in that condition, alone and desolate. She tells us she was ready to shoot up, and was so bad off that it might have just been enough drugs to ruin her for good. "It might have even killed me," she tells us. "But then I couldn't do it. I just felt something or someone was stopping me. Today, I believe that someone was the Lord. Now I am here, and I'm trying to put my life together—a life I almost lost for good. And I thank my God that He found me when I was lost and alone."

Like Zaccheus, these women talk of their experiences of going to great lengths to see Jesus. And they, too, want to make amends as he did. Maybe they won't be giving half of their possessions to the poor, and returning unjust money given to them for taxes, but there will be other ways they will be making restitution for the wrongs they have done. This story now has new meaning in their lives, and never again will Zaccheus be just another name in the Bible.

This is an example of how the gospel comes alive. As we gather to listen to the Word and discuss how it is important to us now, we not only gain new insights, but we are nourished by it. No one said living the gospel would be easy, and certainly this group can vouch for that. New meanings continue to emerge, and lives are changed as we take time to pray the Scriptures. I admit my own faith life has been enriched by these stories and so many others: stories of women who have not lost their faith, even in the worst of situations.

Listening to the Sunday readings in my parish church is no longer a passive event. I realize I will be taking these same words to the detention center in less than twenty-four hours. They need to speak to me and my life before I ask the women to discern how these same words will touch theirs.

As we conclude each session, we pray we can be strong to live the gospel. And we pray that these words can give us strength for the journey. That's all we can ask for now.

Chapter 4

· ·

A DAY IN THE LIFE OF AN INMATE

I

T'S 4:30 A.M. and the lights of the pod are switched on. Time to get up! Breakfast trays will arrive within the next half hour. There will be no food if you decide to sleep in. Yes, it sounds pretty early for breakfast. I know the women would agree on that point. But nobody said life in jail would be easy. Silence permeates the atmosphere as the women partake of their first meal directly off the tray. Having completed their meal, they can return to their beds to catch a little more sleep before the day's activities begin.

During one of our gatherings, we talked about how God could become part of their day, beginning with the earliest hours. Here are some of their responses:

"Because I'm still so tired when I first awake, I'm lucky if I can even mutter a prayer...but I do try to at least thank God for the food before me."

"As I awake, I reach for my Bible and flip it open. I want to start this day right, and for me, that means listening to His word in the Scripture."

"I try to start off each day with a smile and think to myself, "Have a good day today." I praise the Lord for another day and I remind myself not to worry because the Lord will be handling all my problems throughout the day."

"I wake up each day and thank God for another promised day. Then I read 'My Daily Bread,' which has reflections for each day."

When the lights are turned on again at 8:00 A.M., it's time to begin the day's activities. There are the daily routines of showers, shampoos, getting dressed, fixing one's hair and putting on makeup. Even though there's no place special to go, they all agree you just feel better when you can pamper yourself a bit.

With that preparation, they are now ready to begin their day. There are many opportunities for the women to enrich their lives while they are awaiting their trial date. One of the most popular programs for the women is called MATCH (Mothers and Their Children). It was created to help parents improve their parenting skills, as well as allow physical contact with their children through visits. Unless the mothers are enrolled in this program, they are not able to enjoy a contact visit with their children in the MATCH room. And it's not just a matter of signing up for those privileges; it's a matter of commitment—a commitment to attend class for one and a half hours each day from Monday through Friday. In order to have a contact visit with your child(ren), the women must also maintain good behavior in the facility. If they fulfill those requirements, they will have the opportunity to visit with their child(ren) for one hour on the evening the MATCH room is open. Every mother knows how hard it is to be disconnected from her little ones, and these incarcerated women are no different. Over the years, thousands of women have benefited from this wonderful program.

Often, our weekly good news stories are related to a MATCH visit during the previous week. Being reunited with both children and grandchildren—if only for a brief period—can give a mother a reason to change her life when she gets out. Joy at being able to hold her baby or toddler reminds her of her greatest treasure—one she doesn't want to ever lose. Fortunately, most of the children are left in the care of either their grandparents or another family member, and are able to stay connected to the inmate. I remember one of the mothers telling us, "My mother is so good to my kids. She makes it much easier for me to be here. It still hurts to be separated, but at least I know they have someone to hug and kiss them till I return."

It's not uncommon for the older children to be uncomfortable visiting their parents. In fact, there are several pre-teens and teens who just won't come to the jail. They are embarrassed that their mothers are there. And those who do show up often spend that time blaming their parents for ruining their life by not being home with them. After a visit of that nature, no one feels good.

For the most part, however, the weekly visits set up through the MATCH program are a positive experience for both the children and the parents. These women are motivated to become better parents, and willing to do what it takes to make that happen. The classes they must attend focus on good parenting skills: the importance of positive image building, setting priorities, establishing boundaries, etc. One of the women told the group that she was so young when she had her first child that she made a lot of mistakes in trying to raise him. And now that she's attended these classes in parenting, she feels much more confident, and is eager to apply what she's been learning when she is free again.

One evening, I asked to be allowed to observe the mothers interacting with their children during the visiting hour. I was anxious to see how all the principles I had heard about this program really worked. What an experience that was!

The MATCH room is different from every other room in the county jail. The floor has a carpet where the children can sit and play. There are bookshelves filled with children's books and toys. And the room is a large, open space, allowing room for the mothers to sit on the floor and interact with their little ones.

When I arrived, the visiting had already begun and the place was a bit noisy, but it was a good type of noise: talking, laughter, and even singing. Most of the little ones were completely unaware of where they were as they played. All they knew was that Mommy was there, and that was good. The families stayed in their separate groups, only interacting with immediate family members. I watched a mother reading to her toddler while her baby lay asleep on her lap. Another was racing cars with her four-year-old son. And the older ones just sat and talked, giving Mom a chance to listen to what was happening in their lives away from her. I didn't see any tears, but then, I wasn't there when they had to say goodbye.

Later, during one of my sessions with the women, I asked those who had been involved in the MATCH program to tell us what it was like—that one hour with their children. It was a grandmother who first shared her story.

She said, "I had only one son, but he gave me six grandchildren, and for that I am so happy. Four of them came to see me, and they were all very young and close together in age. They couldn't understand why I was wearing these clothes, and why I couldn't go home with them after our visit was over. It felt so good to be able to hold them and tell them how much I loved them. But I must admit, it really hurt when it was over. My son was good about bringing them week after week. I can't wait to go home so I can be with them all the time."

Jenny told us about her experience and what it meant to her. "I never realized how important my children were to me until they were taken away. I don't know what I'd do if I wasn't able to see them periodically. I'll do whatever it takes to keep that connection while I'm here in jail. They are too little to understand why Mommy lives here and not at home. Hopefully, I'll be home before they grow up and do understand."

Even though many teens don't want a contact visit with their mothers, there are exceptions, and Carol's daughters are a good example of this. For months, they had come to see their mother during normal visiting hours in a room separating them by a glass wall. They were able to converse with her over the phone. For them, it wasn't good enough. Carol decided to attend the MATCH classes in order to have a contact visit with them. She was happy to share this experience. "I entered the room and could see their faces through the glass window. The girls were smiling and looked anxious for me to join them. What a reunion! We hugged and held each other for a long time. Tears followed. My one daughter begged me to please come home. Soon school would be starting, and she asked if I could try to be home by then. I told her I was going to try, but I knew it wasn't in my hands. I do have a court date soon. I pray daily that I will soon be free. My daughters need me during these challenging years of their life."

The MATCH program is only one of the numerous opportunities the inmates are given to better themselves. There are classes on computer skills, GED certification, arts and crafts, as well as courses for rehabilitation such as anger management and the 12 step program. And in the area of spirituality, there are sessions of Bible study, sacramental studies, centering prayer, and journaling, to name a few. Almost all of the above classes and programs are conducted by volunteers. When I became a part of the volunteer ministry, I was amazed at the hundreds of others who were already doing this work. In fact, many of them had been part of this system for twenty to thirty years.

No one can complain that nothing goes on in the county jail while they have to bide their time awaiting trail. And yet, there are those who won't be bothered to take advantage of the numerous programs that are offered. They prefer to watch the television all day, or play cards, or just sleep their day away. Maybe that's the only life they know, and they should be pitied rather than blamed. Fortunately, this is only one segment of the population, as can be seen by all the groups scheduled to meet throughout the week, with most classrooms taking in large numbers.

One week, Sara told us why she now attends classes.

"This is my second time here. The last time I was here, which was almost two years ago, I didn't want to sign up for anything. I was mad, and resented the fact I was even here. So I just lay in my bunk or watched TV, and saw the others line up and leave throughout the day. I have to admit I was bored, but I didn't care. I'd get out soon. Well, now I'm back, and I'm not going to make the same mistake twice. I started asking others which classes were good. Maria recommended I come with her to your class. I think I'm going to like it here. I'm also signing up for the computer class and the Bible study group. Why not learn something while I'm here? I was really stupid ignoring this the last time."

The different classes are scheduled to meet throughout the day, from 8:00 A.M. until 4:30 P.M., and from 6:00 P.M. until 8:00 P.M. Meals continue on schedule, as trays are delivered for lunch beginning at 11:00 A.M. There is an opportunity for snacks between meals if they are fortunate enough to have money in their account to buy commissary food. Items like hot chocolate, soups, potato chips, and cookies can provide a welcome break. Our group has talked about how important it is to be sensitive to the needs of others when it comes to extra snacks. Not everyone has money to buy these treats. Little acts of kindness can go a long way in this situation.

I recall one of the women telling me how sharing their snacks can make someone new to the pod feel welcome. This may seem like a small thing to us. After all, we are only minutes from the nearest fast food restaurant. But to a newcomer or someone very lonely, it can be the difference between a good day and a bad one. One day, Shanna told me she had a dream the night before that we were meeting at Starbucks, and she was treating me to one of their fine blends. And she added, "I really hope that dream can become a reality some day." I hope so, too.

Supper trays begin arriving at 4:30 P.M. Although that may seem early for an evening meal, breakfast was served twelve hours ago. All meals are served on plastic trays divided into compartments for the different foods. There are no plates or cups and saucers; the food is placed in the different sections, with a carton of milk added for a drink and plastic wear for utensils. Although there is an attempt to provide a balanced diet, it tends to be heavy on starches. It's not unusual for the women to gain weight while they are in jail.

The evening hours are spent relaxing by watching TV, talking in small groups, playing cards, writing notes, etc. In many of the pods, small groups gather to read the Bible and pray. The women have told me how important this prayer time is for them at the end of a long day. In fact, they often mention they will miss these groups when they eventually leave the jail.

All must be in their bunk bed by 10:00 P.M. and lights are out at 11:00 P.M. Some use this time in bed to read their Bibles or other books for inspiration. One woman said, "If I go to bed with thoughts of God, I sleep better. So I make it a point to read at least something from my Bible before I close my eyes. I hope to continue to do this when I'm back in the free world."

When writing about their thoughts at the close of the day, we can see a strong comparison to their waking moments. To quote in their own words how they end the day:

"I say good night and read my Bible before going to bed. I then reflect upon my life and see how I have made changes for good. I want to change for the good."

"I reflect on my philosophy that after every rain comes a rainbow, and at the end of every rainbow is a pot of gold. Seek that pot of gold; it's God. The beautiful chain reactions are creations of the Lord. They are awesome."

"I lay in bed, wondering what the next day will bring, good or bad. And each night, I pray from my heart and my mind. I pray God hears what I say."

"Everyone says a prayer together at night before we go to bed. I go to my bed early and write, 'Thank you, Jesus' for blessing me with the people he has put in my life through all the chaos of my day."

I was impressed at how much they work at making God part of their day. When I was growing up, one of my spiritual directors encouraged me to try to make a habit of recalling the presence of God throughout each day. I believe these women are trying to do this same thing. And God is truly in their waking moments from dawn until dusk.

Chapter 5

I FOUND GOD IN JAIL

I F WE THINK of sacred moments and places in our lives, we normally focus on a beautiful cathedral, a tranquil lakeside, or a cabin set deep in the forest. Those are the places we can be quiet and alone. We feel the closeness of God. Away from the noise and distractions of the city, the hustle and bustle of the crowd, we are at one with our Creator.

What a contrast to the environment of the incarcerated women at the county jail. And yet, it is this place, with all its noises and distractions, which many have revealed as the place where they found God.

I'll never forget the day Caroline told us how she finally felt at peace and one with God, after years of running away: running from the law, from her faith, from herself. She said:

"I wasn't going to let anyone find me. I knew I was guilty and should serve time, but as long as they couldn't find me, I was free. But I really wasn't free, and now I realize that. Someone warned me the police were coming to my apartment on a drug search. That didn't scare me because I had an escape. When I heard them entering the building, I quickly rolled myself into a long carpet I was storing in the living room. I ended up lying next to the wall with enough space for breathing out of the end of it. It was

31

perfect. I could hear them walking through the different rooms, searching for anything or anyone. Then the door closed, and I could finally pull myself out. But to my surprise, I looked up to see an officer doing a last-minute check. And to his surprise, he found something, I mean someone—me. So here I am, and I have to admit I feel all right. I've finally stopped running, being anxious about what was going to happen next. These past two months I've had time to think, to pray, and to reconnect to God."

She is one of many who have concluded that being in jail has been one of the best things that ever happened to them, because only when they were here did they get their priorities in order. Only here, where everything had been taken from them, did God become an integral part of their life.

And then there was Beatrice, and her repeated trips to the county jail. Each time she was dismissed, she said she was determined to stay away from here. But unfortunately, it was only a matter of time, and she was sitting before me in class again. Now she is ready to leave for rehab in a few days. "I guess for some of us, it just takes longer to get the message," she said to me. "The retreat I just participated in has made an impact on me, and now I feel I am ready, with the added help of rehab, to get my life in order. God is number one. He has touched my heart, and I am ready to reform so I can be reunited with my two children again. I know I'll have the same temptations, but this time I have the added strength of my faith … a faith that I had abandoned for years."

I have watched this young woman struggle over the past years. I remember when she was leaving the last time, how restless she was. I was not surprised to see her return. But this time, I'm looking at a different woman, a woman very much at peace with herself and at one with her God. I pray that the strength and grace she has received will keep her focused as she returns to the free world. During our prayer time, she asked us not to forget her after she is gone, as we place our petitions before God each week. We won't. God go with you, Beatrice.

The majority of the women I meet with each week are mothers. However, every so often there are some grandmothers in the group.

Since I am a grandmother, I can relate to them. And I remember the words this elderly woman spoke one Monday afternoon:

> "After my children were grown and gone," she began. "I felt I had nothing to live for … so I turned to drugs. Now that I've had time to think about it, I realize I have a lot to live for. I look forward to the day I can leave here. I want to become involved with my church. I need God in my life again. And I want to become part of my grandchildren's lives, too."

It would be easy to devote an entire book to multiple stories of women who have thanked God for the opportunity to put their lives in order as they spend time in the county jail. This message, however, will be interwoven into the other chapters of this book as an underlying theme.

Some of the favorite passages for the women to read and reflect upon are found in the Acts of the Apostles in the New Testament. It is here they see the disciples of the Lord preach his Word, both within and outside the jail walls. And even though these women have not been sent to jail for preaching the gospel, they can imitate the disciples in using this place for spreading His Word to others. In Acts 16, we hear of Paul and Silas being thrown into jail in Philippi, accused of disturbing the city and advocating customs unlawful for the Romans. We read:

> About midnight while Paul and Silas were praying and singing hymns to God as the prisoners listened, there was suddenly such a severe earthquake that the foundations of the jail shook; all the doors flew open, and the chains of all were pulled loose. When the jailer woke up and saw the prison doors wide open, he drew his sword and was about to kill himself, thinking that the prisoners had escaped. But Paul shouted out in a loud voice, "Do no harm to yourself, we are all here." He asked for a light and rushed in and trembling with fear, he fell before Paul and Silas. Then he brought them out and said, "Sirs, what must I do to be saved?" And they said, "Believe in the Lord Jesus and you and your household will be saved." So they spoke the word of the Lord to him and to everyone in his house. He took them at

that hour of the night and bathed their wounds; then he and all his family were baptized at once.

—Acts 16:25-35

This is quite a story of evangelization in jail. No wonder the women like it. This is only one of numerous accounts in the early writings of the disciples where they were found within jail walls. If we look throughout history, there are also plenty of examples of conversions within prisons. It's not surprising the same thing happens today.

One of the classes for spiritual renewal focuses on the celebration of the sacraments in the church. Each month, we have the privilege of having one of the local priests come to our session and celebrate a liturgy with the women. It's their one contact with the worshipping community outside the jail, and they always look forward to it.

Father Kevin celebrating the monthly liturgy

Once a year, we have a special liturgy where the sacraments of baptism, confirmation and Eucharist are celebrated. Over the past few years, I have been able to help prepare a number of Catholic women to receive these sacraments. They were usually adults who had been baptized as infants, but were in a situation where they were not prepared for the other sacraments. Now they are ready to continue their journey of faith, and are anxious to learn about the steps needed to receive these other sacraments. We are fortunate to have two local bishops who are retired and available to confer these sacraments when a group of women are ready.

I remember the last time our group witnessed this event. There were six women to be confirmed, two of whom were also receiving Eucharist for the first time. We had begun preparation a couple months earlier, taking time to study the meaning of the sacraments, focusing on how they belong in our lives today. These sessions are open to all Christian women. They are not limited to those of the Catholic faith. This seems to be a good policy, since many have told us how much they have learned about the Catholic religion while attending the classes. In fact, it has given them a new understanding of the church, correcting some of their erroneous impressions. And it also deepened their own appreciation of their Christian baptism.

As we share together, we are able to discover the sacramental moments in their life. For many, it's a time to rededicate their lives to Christ—to begin again. And I notice how the group begins to form their own community of faith as we prepare the candidates for the celebration. A week before the bishop arrives, we have a special prayer service incorporating the prayers, the scriptural readings, and the ritual of the sacrament of confirmation. This helps all of us better participate in the ceremony on the day of the celebration.

The bishop arrives on the scheduled day as the thirty women are gathered in the chapel. Six candidates, proudly wearing a red stole over their prison garb, sit in the first rows of the assembly. As the music begins, the voices of the group fill the room. You can feel the presence of the Spirit amongst us. When the bishop addresses the women who are being confirmed, they respond enthusiastically.

As they are signed and sealed with the holy oils, all eyes are on the candidates. No one is a passive member of the community on that day. I doubt anyone will ever forget it.

Afterward the bishop commented on how impressed he was with this group of women, a group that seemed so aware of what was happening. He said he celebrates this sacrament frequently in parishes throughout the year, but today it was different. They truly participated in the ceremony: listening attentively to the readings, responding to the prayers, and singing with enthusiasm. The grace of God was in that room. I had to agree. I, too, have been part of many celebrations for the sacrament of confirmation over the past thirty years. But this one was different; it was special. It was another sign that God is found where we least expect Him.

After the ceremony, certificates are given to the inmates who received the sacraments. Those who are going home soon will keep them, while others send theirs to their family for safekeeping. Since the jail is within the boundaries of the cathedral, they are signed with the name of the cathedral as the designated church where the reception of the sacrament took place. It's one positive thing these parents, husbands, and children can retain while they await the return of their loved ones. And it's also a sign of hope that these women are on the right path again. I realize how important it is to not only give the incarcerated women encouragement, but to also include their families.

Hardly a week passes without one of the women giving testimony to the fact that it took this turn in her life to show her what was missing. Their faith becomes alive again, and they are ready to change their ways. By coming to classes, this journey of faith is nourished by the ministers and the community gathered to pray. And my own faith is strengthened by their witness of God's grace in their life.

Chapter 6

ALL IN A PILLOWCASE

Inmate walking down hall with pillowcase

REBECCA IS WALKING down the corridor, dragging her pillowcase, which is filled with all her belongings. There are two sheets, one blanket, two towels, one washcloth, three sets of underwear, three pairs of socks, a few toiletries, a notebook and pencil, a few items she created in her arts and crafts class, some commissary foodstuffs, and one Bible. That's it. Except for the clothes on her back, this is the extent of her worldly possessions while she is a resident of the county jail, and it all fits in one pillowcase.

What a contrast to the amount of things the average woman possesses. When we talk about this meager amount of belongings, the women have lots of stories to tell about how creative they become when resources are so limited. Instead of feeling sorry for themselves, they take what little they have and make the best of it. After all, there's no alternative.

One of the things they create is an extra snack from the items they are allowed to purchase in the commissary. The commissary is a small shop, set up in one of the rooms with a half-door opening. Inmates are allowed to purchase small items for their personal use if they have money in their account. There are a few foods, such as soups, cheese, chili, corn chips, cookies, and other small items they can buy for snacks.

Since there are no arrangements for cooking, they have discovered ways to work around the system. They told me how they can make a good cup of soup using tap water. They let the water flow until it's very hot. After they fill the cup with the hot water, they add the soup. Next they place a book over it for a short time. This helps the soup dissolve properly. And then it's ready to be eaten and enjoyed!

One afternoon, after we finished our class time, we had the luxury of time to talk about some of their favorite things, and food came into the conversation. I remembered the story of the hot soup and was curious about other ways they used their meager belongings to create something good to eat. They were anxious to tell me. I quickly jotted down some notes, and I hope I do justice to their recipes below.

Tamales

Smash corn chips and add a little bit of hot water until it becomes doughy. Put chili or melted cheese on it and roll it on a plastic bag until it gets hard. Then enjoy!

Burritos

Take a large bag of nacho cheese flavored tortilla chips and add a bit of hot water. Crush that and make it into masa. Flatten it out while it still is in the bag. After you have flattened the masa, open the bag and put on chili, beans, cheese, or whatever else you like. Fold the masa over, so it becomes similar to a burrito.

Baked Potato

You can make a baked potato with potato chips. Smash the chips and cover them with hot water in the bag until they blend together as a whole. Then add toppings, such as cheese, chili, etc.

There were several other recipes the women talked about, but these few show how creative one can be when deprived of the things we take for granted. However, I doubt any of these creations will follow them back to the free world where the real ingredients are available. But it does indicate that where there's a will—and a commissary—there's a way.

Often the women will tell of how their lives before jail were filled with too much stuff. I think most of us can say that about our own belongings. The American dream seems to suggest that the more we have—the better! A classic example of this is the number of storage rental units that have popped up in every town in the country. In most cases, their purpose is to store the stuff we cannot, or will not, throw away. It's not until it gets taken away that we begin to look at the real value or priority of worldly possessions.

Tania tells us about how the desire for things led to her arrest. "I had everything," she says, "a wonderful husband and two fine children, a good home with nice furnishings, a comfortable life style in the suburbs. But I wasn't satisfied. I wanted more. And so I started writing bad checks, misusing my credit cards, and finding other dishonest ways of getting things without paying for them. I just got greedy. I felt the more I had, the happier I'd be. But I was wrong. I finally got caught, and here I am today. I had to return all the goods, and I still owe my creditors. It was all so stupid."

Tania is fortunate because she has a husband and children who are ready to take her back after she completes her sentence, and she's learned one of life's lessons while she is still young. Things don't bring happiness, especially things we are not entitled to. If she can learn to live with a few material things from a pillowcase, I think she'll be happy with the material things she has, and hopefully her greed will be cured.

It is a fact that the majority of the inmates are serving time because of an addiction. Wanting those things that are not good for them—drugs, excessive alcohol, over-indulgent spending—has left them with only enough items to fill a pillowcase, a real contrast to their previous lifestyle.

However, for some, it began with poverty. They remember their early years as a time of deprivation. Their families lived in a poor neighborhood, and they envied those who wore nice clothes and could eat at fine restaurants. The thought of easy money, a way to get rich quickly, loomed before them. No wonder they fell to the temptation of drugs when it was put before them. In some instances, the whole household became involved in the drug culture. And the family home became the place for the buying and selling of illegal substances.

My heart went out to this mother telling us of her family predicament. It was the week before Mother's Day. She said, "I really feel like I've failed as a mother. My son is sitting on death row because he killed a man involved in a drug deal. My daughters are here with me, awaiting trial because they were part of the same drug operation. And of course, here I sit because I allowed this to happen in my house. When the police came, we were all taken in. What kind of a Mother's Day is this going to be for us?"

Unfortunately, this scenario occurs often. The women will ask for prayers for their husbands, brothers, and boyfriends who are also serving time across the street in the main jail. And who's home taking care of the children? Usually a grandmother or a foster parent.

In the Scriptures, we read how Jesus told us where to put our priorities and how to direct our energies. We read in Matthew's gospel:

> Do not store up for yourself treasures on earth where moth and dust destroy and thieves break in and steal. But store up treasures in heaven where neither moth nor decay destroys, nor thieves break in and steal. For where your treasure is, there also will your heart be.
> —Matthew 6:19-22

Now this passage takes on a real meaning for the inmates. They tell how their focus on owning things has changed, now that they are taken away from them.

Denise says, "It's funny how I no longer think about the latest fashions. I don't even find myself wanting to get to the nearest mall. Just putting on this blue outfit each day is a reminder that I really don't need so many clothes. But I'm not sure I'll ever want to wear blue again, once I'm free. Look for me in bright colors—reds, yellows, and pinks."

Susan adds, "I began to realize how much time I spent worrying about how I looked. Did I have enough makeup on? Were my clothes color-coordinated? What would the others think of me? Now I say to myself, who cares? That's not what brings me happiness. I feel so much more comfortable just being myself here. I don't think I'll be so concerned about clothes again."

Finally, Kathy responds, "When I look at how I can live with so few things, I laugh. I was the one who couldn't get her clothes into her dresser drawers because I had so much stuff. I never thought about it being too much. But now, looking back, it really was. This Scripture passage spoke to me today. Stuff can get in the way. It can mess up our priorities. I think God is trying to tell me something."

I've often thought of what I would do if I had to put everything I needed into one pillowcase. I soon realized my life is cluttered with too much stuff. Maybe I need to do some sorting out and giving away. I need to take to heart this message which I have shared with the women. It is said that when we arrive at heaven's gate, the only things we will have with us are the things we have given away.

Chapter 7

. . . .

ASHES AND OIL AND OTHER GOOD THINGS

Ashes

DUST THOU ART and unto dust thou shall return," recites the minister as he moves through the congregation. These are familiar words, marking the beginning of Lent to all Christians around the world. Fortunately, this ritual also takes place within the walls of the jail.

I had no sooner begun my ministry in our county jail when Ash Wednesday arrived. I looked forward with some anxiety to my first experience of going into the pods where the women resided. Before this day, I had only met the inmates in the chapel room. Now I would be going into their territory, the area they lived in all day, except for the times they were released to attend classes or church services, to take care of business with their lawyer, or visit with a family member.

The volunteers meet to receive our ashes and pray before beginning our rounds to the different units. My friend Anita joins me as we head for the first pod in Unit A. When we arrive, a security button has to be released to open the heavy metal door separating us from the room where the women reside. The clang of the door closing behind us reinforces the fact these incarcerated women are not free.

As we enter the dimly lit room, with its rows of bunk beds and lined up tables, it is obvious this is no five star hotel. But then, this is jail.

We invite anyone who wishes to receive ashes to come forward. Many of the women are still resting in their bunk beds and need encouragement from the other inmates to get up and join the group. Since receiving ashes on Ash Wednesday is a universal custom of almost all Christian churches, we remind them they did not have to be Catholic to participate. This brings a few more women to the group.

We begin by talking about the meaning of the season of Lent. We ask them to think about what they might do differently during the next forty days to prepare for the feast of Easter. Just being incarcerated is a penance, but this doesn't stop them from giving suggestions on little practices of self-sacrifice they can personally add to their daily life. One of the women speaks up, "I know every so often we get a special treat on our meal tray. I think it would be good if I could give that up during Lent. I remember as a child, giving up was always part of Lent in our family." Upon hearing that suggestion, another woman adds, "For me, it would be more important if I gave up using bad language. And from what I hear around me, I think others might consider doing the same." Many in the group nod with this remark.

Before we distribute the ashes, I begin with a prayer asking the Lord to help us during this season in our efforts of self-denial, and to give us His blessings of forgiveness, to which they all respond, "Amen."

Anita then reads a scripture verse from one of St. Paul's letters to the Corinthians (2 Cor. 5:20-6:2), where he implores us to be reconciled with God. The women respond with a prayer from the handout given them for this service.

As each woman steps forward, we place ashes on her forehead and bless each of them by making the sign of the cross while saying, "Turn away from sin and be faithful to the gospel." After all have received their ashes, we concluded with a final prayer and a promise of prayer for all of them during the holy season we are entering. As we depart, many respond with their promise of prayers for us, and with words of gratitude for coming to them on this day. Although they are locked up, they are truly part of the universal church today.

Each year, I return on Ash Wednesday to repeat the beautiful ritual of praying with the inmates and distributing ashes. In most cases, everything flows well by the script, and the women are happy we are there. In fact, this really came home to me recently when I was routinely moving from station to station.

Since I now had access to the women who are isolated in cells and in lockdown, they are usually placed on my list to visit. These women are separated from the larger groups, either because of the crime they committed or some disturbance they caused in the pods. And sometimes it's for their own protection. I didn't want to know why they are there. My ministry is to be there for them.

This particular Wednesday, I accompanied the guard to each doorway while she knocked and inquired if the inmate would like to receive ashes. For the most part, they are not interested; however, periodically the person inside replies in the affirmative. As we are moving down the hall, I hear this voice call out from the back area, "I want ashes," and the next thing I see is a woman stepping from the shower area. The guard quickly tells her to put something on, and we'll come to her. She steps into the open area with a towel draped around her tattoo-covered body and reverently joins me in prayer. I place the blessed ashes on her forehead, and she quickly steps back in to finish her shower. We have not moved out of the area before I hear her voice call, "Hey, wait, come back. I need more ashes; they are all washing off of me!" As I inwardly laugh I shout back, "That's alright, you are still blessed." And I think to myself, the desire for ashes is so great it knows no boundaries.

Blessing with Holy Oil

"Is anyone among you suffering? He should pray. Is anyone in good spirits? He should sing praise. Is anyone among you sick? He should summon the presbyters of the church, and they should pray over him and anoint him with oil in the name of the Lord."

—James 8:13-15

Blessings and oil go hand in hand. They are a tangible sign of the presence of God in the community. And the community at the county jail reaches out for help in their hardships, in their sickness, and in their suffering, be it physical or mental. The smell of the oil, the touching of the senses, all reinforce the care and love these women are seeking.

We attach the use of oil with many of the sacraments of the church. Candidates are blessed and anointed with oil in both the sacraments of baptism as well as confirmation. But these occasions are rare while the women are serving their time in jail. However, there is a time when oil is included in the celebration with the women. It occurs during retreats, as well as during some monthly liturgies.

During the liturgy at the end of the retreat weekend, the priest invites any of the women who would like to be anointed with oil to come forward. He reminds them they do not need to be physically ill to participate. In fact, he encourages them to receive this blessing to be strengthened in their weakness. They usually all respond to the call. I've watched this prayerful experience numerous times, and it affects the entire community. Tears flow, smiles abound, and peace fills the room.

Throughout the year, we look for other opportunities to use oil. Sometimes at the closing of our monthly liturgy, we have extra time to bless the women. Bea and I will each take the holy oil and bless the hands of each inmate as we pray for and with them. I recall after one of these liturgies I overheard two of the women talking about this ritual. One of them said, "I'm not going to wash my hands until I really need to. This wonderful smell reminds me of how much I am loved by God and others."

During Holy Week each year, we set aside one of our usual class sessions to observe the commemoration of the Lord's Passion. We begin with the reading of the Passion, inviting the women to follow with their booklets, participating in the narrative of the crowd. I'm always impressed at how seriously they join in. This past year, when I had explained how we would all take the part of the people, one of the women said, "I'll say most of their parts, but please don't ask me to cry out, 'Crucify Him,' because I just can't."

After the Scripture reading and the numerous prayers for the people of the world, the women come forward to venerate the cross. I remind them that this same action is being performed during Holy Week all over the world, and for at least this moment, they are united with the whole church. Somehow, jail walls no longer separate them.

And when we have finished distributing Communion, Bea and I proceed to take holy oil and bless their hands, reminding them their hands are holy. They are to use these hands to hold their Bible and read the Word, to show kindness to one another, and to spread His message of love. Yes, oil is a sign of God's love, and in the jail's environment it can be a force for goodness and peace.

And Other Good Things

"O God, by whose word all things are made holy, pour forth your blessing upon this wreath and grant that we who use it may prepare our hearts for the coming of Christ," we pray as we gather around the traditional Advent wreath. During this season, we not only remember Jesus' first coming into the world at his birth, but we also celebrate his daily coming into our hearts now, and we anticipate his future coming at the end of time. And it is fitting to bring this ritual into our gathering at the county jail.

Since we are not able to actually light the candles each week while we say the Advent prayer, we use our imaginations as we gather around the unlit candles on the wreath. So many times we learn to improvise because of the regulations limiting the use of certain objects. And that's all right. It's the message and the meaning that is important. The wreath made of evergreens is a sign of God's constant love for us.

One year, we used the Advent wreath as an opening prayer service for the semi-annual retreat. We invited the inmates to think of what they were going to do during this season of waiting to help remind them of His coming into their daily lives. When they were ready, each one stepped into the middle of the room where the wreath was being created and placed her individual branch into the circle to form the community wreath. As we witnessed each person coming forth, we prayed for her, asking God to give her the strength to follow her resolve. Afterwards, several of them told me it was the first time the Advent wreath took on a special meaning in their lives.

There's no doubt that being incarcerated during the holidays is especially difficult for these women. The majority of them are mothers—mothers presently without their babies and children. I remind them to put their attention on the spiritual aspect of the season, and keep their hope alive for the day they will be reunited with their families. I also encourage them to connect to their families through cards or, if possible, a phone call or visit. The reality is that many of their families have disconnected themselves and want little or nothing to do with the family member in jail. It's not uncommon to hear a mother say her children are embarrassed that she is in jail, especially if they are teenagers. When I hear this, I am saddened. I cannot take their pain away, but I can walk with them and show my concern for them, and we join hands and hearts in prayer.

One of the prayer services we use during the Christmas season is called, "Great Day in Bethlehem." It combines the Scripture readings of the Christmas story with the numerous Christmas hymns. I've noticed how much the women enter into the spirit of this program. Songs are sung with great enthusiasm, readings are pondered, and there is at least this one hour to uplift their minds and hearts and feel the peace of the season.

During this same season, we were able to enjoy the one-man presentation of Dickens' Christmas Carol, titled *"Bah Humbug"* and presented to us by Damian Gillen. The women thoroughly enjoyed his interpretation of this timeless classic, as he played everyone's part from Tiny Tim to Scrooge himself. The women laughed, cried, and cheered as this story of hope and compassion touched their hearts. I'm sure they had heard this story before, but never was its message so powerful.

Scrooge interpretation

During other times of the year we have also had Damian present the Word of the Lord through parables. Again, the Scriptures come to life.

Music, too, can be holy. Listening to inspirational songs or singing the verses are both forms of prayer that lift one's mind to God and create an atmosphere of peace. I can recall different occasions when the group singled out one of the inmates with an unusually good voice and asked if we could have a solo from her during our closing prayer service. As we listen to a beautiful voice lead us, I am reminded of how good it is to use our gifts to glorify the Lord.

There are many ordinary things we can make holy ... ashes, oil, palm branches, holly leaves, dramas, and so on, but greater than all of these things is the gift of each person. No matter what crime or accusation brings these women into the county jail, they are not criminals in God's eyes. How can we treat them any less than our loving Father?

Chapter 8

LET ME WASH YOUR FEET

THE ROOM IS buzzing with chatter—sounds of excitement and anticipation. It's Thursday evening, and the beginning of a special retreat weekend for thirty incarcerated women. It's also the introduction to life inside the county jail for a group of fifteen women from one of the local parishes who have come together as a team to lead this retreat. For many of these volunteers, it's the first time they have ever been inside a jail. When they agreed to be part of the weekend, they had truly taken a leap of faith. All had experience leading other parishioners in a similar type of retreat, but they knew this group would be different. They have prayed that they will be a source of hope and inspiration to the women who are about to enter the room.

Suddenly the group is outside the door and ready to enter. The team lines up on each side of the room and begins singing, "This is holy ground ..." as the women enter and take a seat in the chairs placed in a large circle around the room. Sister Teresa welcomes everyone. For the most part they have no idea what the next three days will bring.

Because of the limitation on the number of participants, priority is given to those who are already attending one of the weekly spiritual growth classes. These are women who have shown they are making a sincere effort to change their lives. They can be from any Christian denomination, even though the women leading the retreat are all from the Catholic community. Everyone in the retreat group has put in a request to be there, and they feel privileged to be included on the final list. Since this retreat is held twice a year, other inmates who have experienced it often encourage their friends to sign up.

The first evening sets the tone for the following days. There is an ice-breaker to give the inmates an opportunity to get to know each other as well as the group of volunteers. There is time for singing, lots of singing, to keep the theme alive over the next two days. And finally, there is time for praying together.

The ice-breakers are fun activities to help everyone relax. One popular activity is the M&M game. During this game, each person takes a different colored M&M. After selecting a color, the retreatant must introduce herself and do the assigned activity for that particular color. The activities vary from telling your favorite food or hobby to singing your favorite song. As expected, everyone hopes they don't pick the song color because few people are comfortable singing solo. However, they often find creative ways to avoid a solo, and lots of laughter lightens the atmosphere.

Music is a key element in connecting the different stages of the retreat and moving from one activity to another. Having a good guitarist is a key element for setting the mood of the retreat. Once the icebreaker is completed, the guitarist brings us together in song. The retreat team leader, who is responsible for keeping the activities moving on schedule, introduces herself and explains the theme for the upcoming days. She also gives a short history on this type of retreat experience. The final activity of the first evening will be a short prayer service consisting of prayer, reflection, and Scripture based on the chosen theme.

When the women depart, they are reminded to continue in the spirit of prayer and silence until they join us the next morning. The team then gathers for a few minutes of evaluation and planning. There is a sigh of relief that all is going well. Their anticipated fears of the unknown are diminished with their first contact with the inmates. Now they look forward to the next morning, and the full day of planned activities. Finally, the volunteers are escorted from the building after determining the tasks for the next day. Everyone agrees the Spirit is alive and with us.

At 7:30 A.M. on Friday morning, the team awaits the arrival of the women making the retreat. Soon the music begins and smiling faces are seen all around as the group assembles. Everyone is already feeling more at home in these unusual surroundings. After an opening prayer service, the women are invited to break into small groups around the various tables. Each table accommodates six inmates and two team members. This small group will begin to form their own community over the next hours together. The first project they'll do together is decide on a name for their table and design a small poster depicting that name. It's always amazing to see the creativity sparked by this activity. On one of our last retreats, some of the names chosen and illustrated were: Women of Light and Peace, Fire of Love, Light of the Lamb, Family of God, and Lamb of God. Suddenly they are not identified with a number but are given a name, a name with dignity.

The morning hours are filled with testimonies by a retreat team member, followed by discussions at the group tables. This gives the inmates an opportunity to apply the message of the speaker to their own lives. Lots of listening is done by the team members.

It's so important the women have an opportunity to be heard and listened to with respect. Once they have been given ample time to share at their individual tables, representatives are invited to come forward and present their table's reflections to the entire gathering. During the initial presentations, it's obvious some of the women have leadership skills and are comfortable speaking before large audiences. What's interesting to see is how the more timid and introverted ones grow in confidence as the weekend progresses.

Between the first two presentations, we take time for a coffee and cookie break. This is a real treat for the women, because the cookies have been homemade by the ladies leading the retreat. And even though there is enough for everyone, most team members give their share to the inmates when they see how much it means to these women. In fact, one of the ladies said, "I just can't believe I'm in jail. Not only are you filling us with spiritual food, you haven't forgotten our other needs. This is just great! I wish everyone could be here with us in this room today. I feel so lucky."

At lunch time, sandwiches are brought into the room, making it easier to keep to the schedule. The same lunches are also given to the volunteers. It's a good reminder that we are on this journey together. Although food at the jail is nothing fancy, it does provide the nourishment needed for daily living. I remember Sandra saying, "Being in here makes you appreciate and look forward to how good it will be some day to be able to cook your own meals again, or better yet, go out to a restaurant."

The morning concludes with one more testimony from a team member and an opportunity for sharing, a chance to apply the message to your own life. One of the inmates remarked, "I can't believe how much pain has been part of these good women's lives. They all look so happy, and yet when they tell of how they were abused or abandoned by someone they loved, you realize everyone has hardships in life. I tend to look at all the people who come to minister to us as folks who have it together. Listening to these women has opened my eyes to the real world. I'm so grateful to be part of this retreat group. And I want to thank the ladies for being so honest with us today."

The afternoon takes on a different theme, beginning with a service of forgiveness and reconciliation. Tables are cleared and the women gather in a circle where they can focus on the theme of forgiveness. There's music, Scripture readings, and prayers, including a rite for recalling their weaknesses and asking forgiveness. Although each retreat group creatively works out how this ritual is presented, the overall theme remains the same—seeking forgiveness. Sometimes team members distribute pieces of clay to each of the women and ask them to knead the clay into a form or figure while they recall their weaknesses, failings, and sinfulness. Other times they watch a Team member dramatize the scripture of the Woman at the Well and listen as she talks to them about their experience. Watching their faces as she speaks to them, you are suddenly transported into a different time and place.

Woman dramatizing Scripture

The inmates are invited to respond to this dramatization by writing on small pieces of rice paper something they are sorry for and want to change in their lives. These papers are made of a substance that dissolves when placed in water. One by one, they place their paper into the water and watch it disappear—a reminder of how God forgives us.

No matter what form the service takes, the focus is on repentance and forgiveness. It is a vivid representation of how our sins are taken away. Everyone is invited to participate in this prayerful experience.

The final phase of this reconciliation service takes place with priests and other spiritual leaders. The priests come from nearby parishes for the sacrament of reconciliation and individual counseling. The women who are not Catholic are also encouraged to meet and talk to one of the priests. It's a good opportunity for seeking advice and help in their struggles. The incarcerated women may also choose to speak with one of the members of the retreat team. They can sit with them in a quiet corner of the chapel, or meet in another room near the chapel. While this is happening, an atmosphere of quiet and reflection prevails. It is during these moments that lives are changed and transformed through the power of prayer and the sacraments.

The final meal break is for supper, which is any time after 4:30 P.M. This time, the women will return to their pods for a meal while the retreat team prepares the rooms for the evening's activities. There will be two separate rooms set up: one for the foot-washing and the other for the agape meal. Because of the restrictions on materials brought onto the jail premises, these activities are adapted from the more elaborate presentations given on a parish retreat. With a little creativity and many hands, the proper atmosphere can be created even in a barren room in the county jail.

Chairs are set up in a large circle around the perimeter of the room. An appropriate centerpiece is created in the center of the room. (On one retreat, candles were arranged in the form of a cross with greenery placed around them.) The lights are dimmed and soft music plays. The room is ready.

The inmates arrive in silence at the entrance to the room. They are quietly shown to their places while the retreat team members wait in their places. After all are seated, the reading begins.

... so, during the supper, fully aware that the Father had put everything into his power and that he had come from God and was returning to God, he rose from supper and took off his outer garments. He took a towel and tied it around his waist. Then He poured water into a basin and began to wash the disciples' feet and dry them with the towel around his waist. He came to Simon Peter, who said to him, "Master, are you going to wash my feet?" Jesus answered and said to him, "What I am doing, you do not understand now, but you will understand later." Peter said to him, "You will never wash my feet." Jesus answered him, "Unless I wash you, you will have no inheritance with me." Simon Peter said to him, "Master, then not only my feet, but my hands and head as well." Jesus said to him, "Whoever has bathed has no need except to have his feet washed, for he is clean all over; so you are clean, but not all." For he knew who would betray him; for this reason he said, "Not all of you are clean."

So when he had washed their feet and put his garments back on and reclined at table again, he said to them, "Do you realize what I have done for you? You call me 'teacher' and 'master' and rightly so, for indeed I am. If I therefore, the master and teacher have washed your feet, you ought to wash one another's feet. I have given you a model to follow, so that as I have done for you, you should also do. Amen, amen I say to you, no slave is greater than his master nor any messenger greater than the one who sent him."

—John 13:3-17

The women are directed to remove one of their shoes and socks, and without further words, members of the retreat team pair off and begin to wash the feet of the inmates. Music is played in the background to create the proper mood for this activity. As water is poured upon feet, tears come forth from both retreatants and team members. And sometimes words of encouragement and love are shared. After they complete the circle, it's not unusual for one of the women making the retreat to take the bowl of water and repeat the foot washing for the women who have just washed their feet. This scripture passage becomes a reality.

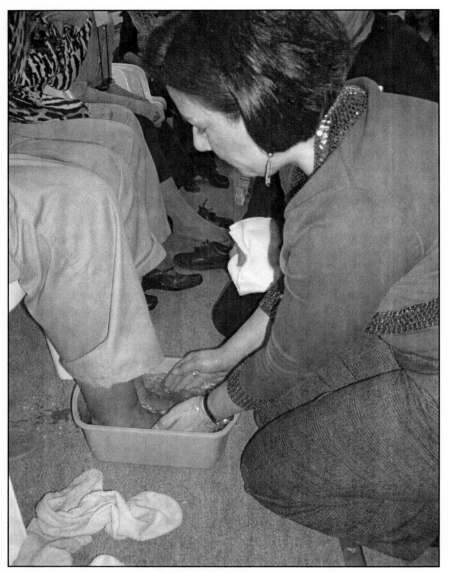

Washing of inmates feet

At the conclusion of this first part of the evening's ritual, the group moves down the hall for the second part of the evening's events: the sharing of the agape meal. In moving from one part of the jail to another, the other inmates look on in wonder at what is happening. There is a sense of order, of prayer, and dignity about these women, and it doesn't go unnoticed.

The retreat leader stands in the doorway of the room for the agape meal. The tables are set and ready. Baskets of bread are on the head table. Carafes of grape juice are at each table, ready to be served. Each one's place has been set with a decorated place mat, an invitation, a music pamphlet, plus a glass and napkin. Many times, the placemats are created by local school children with a message of love and hope. The tables are also decorated with candles, fresh flowers, and sprigs of leaves or holly. The atmosphere is set for the celebration to begin.

As the women walk into the room, their eyes shine and their smiles widen. "All of this is for us," one whispers. As the retreat team leader stands by the door, she welcomes each person by name. She invites them to please join us at the banquet prepared for them. And while they are being seated, the other women on the team are standing around the sides of the room. They are welcoming the women with the uplifting song, "Don't let anyone ever tell you, you are less than beautiful ..." The air is filled with anticipation. No one can imagine what will happen next.

After the women are all seated, Sister Ellen begins by giving an explanation of agape:

> "The meaning and significance of agape is this: agape comes from the Greek word meaning love. It is a very special kind of love. It is unconditional love. It's not the love of mother, father, brother, sister, spouse, or friend, but it's specifically God's love. Tonight we are going to experience God's love in a special way. In this room, at this moment, we are going to relive the Last Supper, that moment in time when Jesus ate his last Passover meal with His apostles. Tonight we are those apostles."

One of the team members continues with a reading from the gospel of John of another meal Jesus shared with his friends:

> When they had finished eating, Jesus said to Simon Peter, "Simon, son of John, do you love me more than these?" "Yes Lord," he

said, "you know that I love you." Jesus said, "Feed my lambs." He then said to him a second time, "Simon, son of John, do you love me?" He answered, "Yes Lord, you know that I love you." Jesus said, "Tend my sheep." He said to him the third time "Simon, son of John, do you love me?" Peter was distressed that He had said to him a third time, "Do you love me?" and he said to him, "Lord you know everything; you know that I love you." Jesus said, "Feed my sheep."

—John 21:15-18

After a song is played, the women are invited to get comfortable, close their eyes, and think of nothing. Just relax. While they sit quietly, they are asked to picture themselves sitting at that same table with Jesus, listening to Him speaking to them, asking for their love.

The dialogue continues as Patsy, one of the team members, reminds them of the importance of this meal they have come to share. She begins:

> "This agape love that God gives us is also the love we are called to show to one another. One of the most meaningful actions of agape love the early Christians shared was the meal eaten together; the bread broken and the cup shared. Then they took the bread and cup—God's agape—and gave it to one another. What we will do here today is a symbolic breaking of the bread and sharing of the cup. This is a commemoration of the Last Supper. There is no Eucharist or Communion."

Soft instrumental music is played while the bread is passed and the grape juice is served. The meal has begun. It may not be a banquet in our eyes. There are no large platters of food to share, and no fine wines to drink. But for these women, on this day, it is a banquet: a feast of love, an agape.

After all have had time to eat, drink, and enjoy each other's companionship, the retreat leader steps forth. She reminds us that at the last supper, when Jesus and his friends got together to share a meal, there was also conversation going on. "We want to take this opportunity for you to share with us anything that is touching your heart now. Or maybe you'd like to share how you personally experienced Jesus on this retreat.

Without any hesitation, they begin. In every group, the extroverts get the conversation started. Cindy jumps up from her seat. It's obvious she's anxious to respond.

"Wow!" she exclaims. "I just can't believe what is happening here. I've never felt so much love in all of my life. It's like you can feel it in the air around us. So much in me wants this to go on and on. To keep singing, and laughing, crying, and praying with these wonderful ladies. I'll never be able to say thank you enough for all you have given to me these last two days. I could go on for the next half hour with my words of appreciation, but I'd better sit down and let someone else talk."

What more could the team ask for? Such sincerity, such gratitude. Once Cindy opened the door with her comments, others followed, all expressing love and sincere gratitude for this retreat experience.

I'll never forget when Maria spoke. She was a very shy person. During the discussions, she listened carefully but seldom said anything. As she hesitantly stood up, she began:

"I can't believe I'm doing this. I've never spoken in public. In fact, I think most of you know I am a very shy person." Everyone nodded in agreement. She continued, "I hope I can make it through this without crying. I just need to tell you this is the first time in my life I have felt loved by someone else. And it's the first time I have begun to feel good about who I am. When I was a young child, my parents told me I was a mistake, that they didn't want more children. I didn't want to be a burden, but I always felt like I was. Then when I was a young adult, this man told me he loved me and he would take care of me. I believed him. But I was wrong. He just used me, and before I realized it, I was helping him with his drug ring. And look what that got me. It took coming to this retreat, meeting these wonderful ladies, to find out about love. Thank you, each one of you for loving me—a stranger. You took me in and accepted me with all my weaknesses. You showed me how God loves me by the way you have loved me."

Father Carl talking to the group

And then the tears on this young woman began to flow.

This agape meal—this love feast—was filled with that sentiment. I recall that it was during that celebration I made a commitment to make every effort to be a part of this meaningful gathering each year.

Soon it's time to end the day's activities. The women return to their pods filled with joy, hope, and enthusiasm. And the rest of us return to our homes, filled with the same sentiments.

The final day of retreat begins with morning prayer. The inmates are anxious to tell us about the reactions of the others when they returned the night before. It reminds me of the story of the woman at the well. They are so filled with the Lord, so ready to spread the good news.

We conclude the weekend with a liturgy led by the chaplain, Father Carl. By this time, everyone is familiar with the music and there is enthusiastic participation. He invites the women to share their thoughts on the gospel during his homily. They are anxious to do so. The inmates are also invited to participate as readers, proclaiming the Word. The community is alive!

And when it's time to bid farewell, it is hard for everyone. The women in the jail have formed a bond with this group of volunteers. They want to continue to be able to support each other. For security reasons, no one is allowed to exchange telephone numbers or addresses. However, they can write letters using either the detention center address or their local parish listing. I always pray that some do.

Soon they are escorted back to their pods, to return to the daily routine of jail life. It's time to come down from the mountain.

Chapter 9

COMING DOWN FROM THE MOUNTAIN

THE STORY OF Jesus transfigured on the mountain sets the stage for the time after the retreat. The words and actions of the disciples reflect the responses of the women: let us stay here; we don't want it all to end. As we read in Luke's gospel,

> …he took Peter, James and John and went up onto a mountain to pray. While he was praying, his face changed in appearance and his clothes became dazzling white. And behold two men were conversing with him—Moses and Elijah, who appeared in glory and spoke of his exodus that he was going to accomplish in Jerusalem. Peter and his companions had been overcome by sleep, but becoming fully awake, they saw his glory and the two men standing with him. As they were about to part from him, Peter said to Jesus, "Master, it is good that we are here; let us make three tents, one for you, one for Moses and one for Elijah.
> —Luke 9:28-33

The women experiencing the retreat say, "How good it has been for us to be here. Can't it just continue?" Reality hits as the sheriff accompanies these women back to their pods. They, too, must come down from the mountain. They must return to their regular routine.

In the weeks to follow, some will gather to study and pray with other inmates who joined them on the retreat weekend, while others will leave to begin their sentence at a state prison. Others will be freed and allowed to go home. No matter where they find themselves, they will be able to keep the spirit of the weekend alive in their minds using the materials they received during the retreat. Sometimes we are able to give each inmate a book entitled *Coming Down from the Mountain* to assist them in this journey.

But before we part ways, before they are led away, we ask the women to share with us in a letter what the days of retreat have meant for them. It is through their own words that we understand how powerful an experience this has been. Later, copies of these letters are given to the team members as a thank you for giving of their time.

After reviewing letters from several retreats, I noticed each retreat reflected a definite theme of gratitude: gratitude for being selected to participate in the weekend, for the powerful effect of the music, for the selflessness of the volunteers, and for the concern of the children who sent letters and cards. They also echoed an appreciation for all they had learned, along with a strong desire to change their lives. Throughout this chapter, this theme of gratitude will be evident in the words written in their letters.

We'll begin by focusing on words of appreciation for being invited to participate in the retreat. The number of the participants is determined by the size of the room, therefore not everyone who wants to attend the retreat is able to come. Priority is given to those who are attending one of the weekly faith sessions, such as spiritual growth, journaling, scripture study, and the sacramental preparation program. Those attending these sessions who wish to participate in an upcoming retreat submit their names. Since the number requesting to come always exceeds the amount allowed in the room, names are drawn using a lottery, or are chosen by the leaders of the classes. It is obvious those selected feel honored and privileged.

Alicia writes, "I am so glad I was chosen this weekend to be here with all these beautiful women of God. I know it wasn't by coincidence—it was God's true calling for me to be here. I thank Him for sending His servants to come and show us the true love of God. I am so happy and I know deep in my heart I too want to be a servant of the Lord, Jesus Christ."

A grateful volunteer retreat group

Roseanne adds, "I got to go to this retreat. I was waiting for so long because I did not get to go in December. I was so happy that my name was picked."

Connie echoes those same sentiments, "I feel truly blessed that I was one of the women chosen to attend this retreat. I look forward to all the happiness and peace that is still to come through our Father God."

Natia's words also have a providential overtone as she writes:

"I know there was a reason for me being one of the lucky people chosen to come to this marvelous retreat. God is calling me.

He wants me to open my heart and let His love overtake me. I have this beautiful feeling inside of me. It's awesome! ... Before this retreat I kept saying I was in jail and also in prison. Jail is where I can see and touch the bars, but my prison was the bars surrounding my heart. And I thank each and every one of you for helping to unlock the prison door in my heart."

There's no doubt Miriam saw God's hand in being chosen. She tells us:

"I know it was God's will for me to come here. Let me explain why. I attend MATCH class for contact visits with my babies. I haven't seen them for about three weeks now. My mom was finally going to bring them so I could spend some time with them. On Thursday, our MATCH officer told me, 'You can either see your children or go on the retreat.' This was a hard decision to make, because I know God comes first. But I had been waiting to see my babies and spend some time with them. So as I sat in the MATCH room I started talking to God and asked Him to give me a sign. I wanted so much to be here, but I also wanted so much to be with my children. I went back to my pod and sat at my table. All of a sudden, I jumped up and called my Bible teacher, who I never call early in the morning. She tells me, 'I have some good news for you. Your little brother who was waiting to be sentenced in May is going to be sentenced tomorrow.' I took this as my sign. So here I am. I didn't get to spend time with my babies, but I got to spend a lot of time with God—and I loved it. I would do it all over again."

To be chosen, to be able to walk this journey of faith, is certainly not taken for granted, as these women have reiterated in their letters. And once entering into the retreat, certain factors contribute to making it more meaningful. One of these is music. We have always been fortunate to have guitarists lead us in song as well as play music to accompany different exercises, and all the women are encouraged to join in the singing.

Krista explains how the music brought peace to her. "This weekend gave me so much peace. A peace that is so unimaginable.

Last night was the first night I have slept with so much comfort and serenity in the six months I have been here. The music has so much love and so much joy that my soul was lifted up. I can now say that I am at peace."

Colleen agrees, as she says, "The music that played through my ears filled me with so much peace, happiness, freedom, and most of all love. I thank God for the beautiful music that can touch our hearts in such a magical way."

"The kind of music I heard this weekend was real music for the soul," writes Rosita. "It's music in which your heart and soul can grow. Music which made you think of others and how they felt. Music which made you remember why God put us here. And most of all, I heard music in which every lyric says God loves me. Thank you for the great music."

Gratitude pours forth for the music and for those who bring the music into the otherwise quiet and somber room during the weekend. These are the women who give of their time to not only prepare for this retreat, but also to present their testimonies during the three days. The incarcerated women are taken aback by such generosity. As Judy recalls, "These women, our sisters, were all such beautiful women—truly angels, hearts so big, so kind and gentle … It was such a beautiful time they shared with us. The time they took from their busy lives, from their families, to come and share the love of Jesus, and their love also with us—you can only imagine. An event I will truly never forget for the rest of my days …God bless each of you and you will forever be in my thoughts and prayers."

Lilian adds, "Little did I know the many surprises you had for me, Lord. You've given me new friends with these beautiful sisters and my new Christian sisters alike … Thank you for bringing the sisters here and pruning our branches for us to grow anew and spread the word wherever we go."

The importance of the message of "passing it on" comes through Nancy's letter as she states, "Each one of us can make a difference just the way each one of you wonderful women have. And if each of us can help just one other person and each one of them helps bring another person to Jesus and so on, can you imagine the impact it can have on the world?"

Natashia agrees on the need to continue the chain of love saying, "I felt unconditional love from every team member and the rest of the girls here. I want to feel this love for the rest of my life. And also be able to give this love to people on the wrong path."

The gratitude flowing from the hearts of the women serving time in the jail touches the women on the team who have come to share this weekend with them. When they read words like, "… most of all I was awestruck by the love manifested from the sisters in Christ …" and "Jesus, I want to thank you for all the angels you sent to be here to guide us through this journey," it makes them glad they came.

For many of the volunteers, it's the first time they have ever been in a county jail. There is usually a mixture of anxiety and fear as they step into the unknown. But it is obvious from the letters of gratitude that those feelings quickly disappear as they put their trust in the Lord, and welcome the inmates as He would do. And it's a grace-filled moment when the women come together. From that first moment onward, each of their lives is changed. Touched by the openness and sincerity of the incarcerated women, the gospel takes on new meaning: to visit the imprisoned becomes a reality.

Over the weekend, lives are changed. The women grow in their knowledge and understanding of the Scriptures through the prayers, study of the Word, and the testimonies of both the team members and women in jail. On one particular retreat, almost all of the participants commented on how much they had learned.

Sabrina writes, "I've learned that through prayer and meditation my faith grows stronger. I have heard so many times this weekend that I am beautiful and I am starting to believe I am beautiful! I have learned that God's Word is food for my soul. That God's Word brings peace and joy to my heart and most important—a smile to my face. I have learned that these women know my hurt and pain and it gives me hope that Jesus can change me. I've learned that God hears my cry … that God loves me … and that I can love myself."

"I have learned I have to forgive to grow and that there are others around me that share my sadness, anger, pain, love, hope, joy, and now peace," replies Maria. "I have learned that I am beautiful and at last I can look at my reflection and like what I see. And I have learned to be honest with my feelings—that it's okay to have an opinion that's different from everyone else. I'm no longer a follower—I'm now a leader for Jesus Christ."

Nora realizes the Lord has a plan for her as she tells us, "I learned to love myself and to love others. To forgive in order to be forgiven. Not to ever lose faith in the Lord Our Savior. I know now the Lord does have a plan for me. I have been chosen by name and I pray I can now stay on the right path."

Barbara also sees a new vision for her life, "I know what I want to do now," she says. "I want to walk with God. I feel like I'm glowing. I want to tell the whole world that God is here. I learned that there are a lot of very good people in the world and a lot of happiness without drugs and alcohol. I can be happy on my own. I don't need drugs."

After a weekend of intense prayer and meditation, numerous women testify to a change taking place in their focus. No longer are drugs, money, power, alcohol, and other negative forces their primary concern. God has become the focal point of their life.

"Just because we are here, does not mean we cannot have hope," says Teresa. "To start new again I feel He is with us all the way. He is telling us that with Him in our hearts, we shall not be afraid … This retreat also showed us that loving one another is one way of showing God we are listening to Him and wanting to be His followers."

Melissa shares that same optimism as she tells us, "I now feel I will have a long and happy life. Like God took away all my worries and fears and made them disappear. And now that I have a new life, everything will be alright—no matter what."

As I watch these women change over the three days, I am not surprised to hear what an impact this experience is having on their lives. Annie's words confirm this in her letter. She writes:

"This weekend has turned me around. I am no longer in darkness. I see only light. I have felt God in the inner most part of my heart. What I didn't learn in thirteen years of schooling, I learned in one short weekend. So many things that this paper is too small to contain them. Some of the strongest points I will remember are how I must forgive myself and it's OK to do that. And I can ask my children and my family for forgiveness and they will. I know now that I can walk in God's path. I am God's child and He will take my right hand and lead me. But the most important thing I learned this weekend is I am worthy of God's love. I share His love and I have never been more sure of anything like I am sure that God loves me!"

Susan's words also reflect a change in her as she tells us, "This retreat has opened my eyes. When my Dad came to see me he said I had that glow again. Praise God because I haven't had the "glow" in months since my brother was murdered. This has opened my eyes again and helped me face reality."

There's no doubt that Shandra's life is heading in a new direction. She shares with us,

"This has been one of the most tremendous experiences in my 44 years on this earth. The brick wall that I had built around me is crumbling because of all the love and wisdom that I've been blessed with. I will always have such a joyous and peaceful easy feeling when I look back and reflect on the faith and love I have felt, shared, cried, and cared with these sisters in Christ. I want to thank you God for being such a forgiving God. I now have a stronger foundation in which to start building my new life with You."

As the volunteers read these letters, their hearts are touched. No amount of money can replace the rewards they gain through the words on these pages. How true it is in giving that we receive.

A final word of gratitude comes from the mouths of children. Although there are no children physically present during the retreat days, they are able to become part of the environment in several ways. School children were asked to create cards for a group of women who would be making a retreat. They were told these women didn't have their own children with them. And these cards would make them happy. They were not told the women were in jail. It was obvious these notes of love touched the hearts of the recipients. Many were moved to tears.

For one of the retreats, a group of sixth-graders created a quilt filled with prayer squares. The quilt had a prominent place. It hung on the wall as a constant reminder to the women. Someone was praying for them.

The children achieved their goal, as Doris writes, "Thank you my children for sharing your hearts with me. You just don't know how much it means to me that little people like yourself have a big caring, loving heart. All of you have touched me in a different way. I am a grandma and when I read and saw the pictures, they reminded me of my own grandson."

And Alicia responds, "To the little children who sent me a card and wrote you love me. Thanks for your cards and your warm words. It made me feel so good inside. And it made me think of my own son. He's 13 years old and this will be my first Christmas without him. I really am going to miss that joy on his face. But your cards lifted my spirits knowing a child of God wrote me and sent me a card … May God bless you and your families."

The gratitude continues as Tina says, "Thank you to the youngsters who, knowing nothing about us, sent their thoughts, taking time out of their young lives to brighten ours."

One of the retreats took place during Advent, a couple of weeks before the feast of Christmas. Valerie expresses how the children helped her at this time. "Thank you for helping us feel close to home during the holidays. Your letters, the words inside of the cards reminded me so much of my son it made me fill up with tears. But don't worry they were happy ones …"

It's never easy to be separated from your family. Liz understands this, but tells us how this retreat helped her. "I've experienced the best Christmas I've had being alone. This is the first time without my family but yesterday I felt like I was with my family. And I just thank you so much for what you did."

These are but a few of the hundreds of letters inmates write after the retreat weekend. But the message is loud and clear. Within three days, lives are changed. New challenges await. And as much as we'd like these days to go on forever, to build our tents and stay, it's time to come down from the mountain; it's time to put our ideals into action.

Chapter 10

WILL YOU PRAY WITH ME?

I GREW UP IN a church of people who did a lot of praying for others. I remember as a child hearing my parents say they were praying for Aunt Florence because she was ill, or for Uncle Bill who was dying. I remember the Sisters at school asking us to pray for the conversion of Russia. There was the pastor who stood in the sanctuary of the big church and led the faithful in prayer. And so it was only natural that I, too, would take care of everyone who was in need by praying for them: praying at night before I went to bed, praying with my family at meals, and of course, praying with the whole church community at the celebration of the Eucharist.

What I find interesting as I now look back on those early years of my life is how comfortable it was to be able to help others just by promising them you would pray for them. You had that feeling you had done your part in making things better—the illness and pain, the world's problems, even your personal anxieties. And maybe you had. Our God is a very understanding Being who looks at our heart and intentions.

However, it wasn't until many years later I came to understand that, as important as it is to pray *for someone* (and it is), it is probably more important to pray *with someone*. And it wasn't until I became involved in jail ministry that these words took on flesh.

Along with my weekly meetings with a group of women, I am also available for one-on-one visitation and counseling. This gives me an opportunity to spend quality time with only one person. For an inmate to receive this counseling, she must fill out a request slip: a green form. These requests are then given to the chaplain or placed in the volunteer room where they can be picked up by the appropriate people.

When I received my first request for a counseling session, I was a bit apprehensive. Even though I had spent years in parish work where I had done counseling, this was different. We would meet in a small room set aside for this purpose—no formal office, no large meeting room, just two chairs in a corner of an office or two small stools set in a long narrow room, whatever was available.

As I await Cynthia's arrival, the young woman who had asked to see me, I pray to the Spirit for guidance. I'm not a counselor by profession and I certainly don't want to say the wrong thing. Soon she appears and I welcome her with a big smile, letting her know I'm happy to be here for her. I've never met this woman before. She isn't in my group session, but apparently one of the other inmates told her about me and encouraged her to ask for me. This gave me a feeling of confidence. She begins talking immediately. I soon realize these women need someone to listen to them, to care about them. I can do that.

She begins by telling me what a hard time she has been having. She was getting both frustrated and discouraged. In fact, she had even considered ways of ending her life. When one of her friends noticed her unhappiness, she suggested that she sign up for a time to see me, that maybe I could help her out of her misery. I believe God works in all of us, and that day He was working through her neighbor in the pod.

The longer Cynthia talks, the more she opens up to me. I listen. It's obvious the man she married had made life difficult for her. Her self-worth was extremely low. Since she has been at the county jail she has had time to rethink her values, and has come to believe she can only make it if he is out of the picture. Unfortunately, his parents now have custody of their two young children, since he is also serving time across the street at the men's unit of the jail. They were both involved with drugs. They were arrested on the same day.

She continues telling me her story for about a half hour. Then she stops and looks at me with tears in her eyes and asks, "Will you pray with me?" I have never before in all my forty-some years of ministry been asked so directly to turn to God at the moment and pray. We bow our heads in prayer and each of us petitions God to help Cynthia: help to turn her life around, to be strong in accepting what the future brings, and courage to make it just one day at a time.

Praying with inmate

Cynthia and I continued to meet weekly for a few more sessions, and she joined our weekly church group. The good news is that, after she was released from jail, she spent a period of time at the Woman at the Well House. This is a home for women needing a place to stay after being released from jail or prison. She divorced her husband and was given back her children. You will see how she has changed her life in the letter she writes in Chapter 15.

Sharon Returns

I was surprised one day to see a request slip from Sharon, one of my former students. She had left my class almost three years ago to serve her sentence at the state prison. When she said goodbye after our last class, I thought that would be the last time I'd ever see her. And so when I received this notice, I had mixed feelings. I knew it would be nice to reunite, but I really was hoping she was finally free.

Sharon held a special place in my volunteer life because she was part of the very first class I taught. I felt ill-at-ease in the beginning, even though I had spent most of my adult life as a teacher. This was different. When I accepted the invitation to lead a group of women, I agreed to do it as long as I could have an assistant. There's always strength in numbers, and I wasn't sure I could go it alone. I was grateful when my friend Anita offered to help me. But as the weeks of meetings progressed, Anita's health declined and I found myself leading the group alone more than I liked.

That's where Sharon came in. She became my right hand helper—setting up the CD player or the DVD on the television, handing out the papers, collecting the booklets, arranging the chairs—doing all those mundane tasks that take time and energy. She was always the first in the room, ready to set up, especially when I was the only teacher. I began to depend upon her. When she was ready to leave for state prison, I found myself wanting her to stay. Of course, that was not going to happen, nor should it. Others did step up to help when she left us, and I began to become more comfortable with anyone stepping forth. But I never forgot Sharon and how she helped me help others.

Now that she was back, I was anxious to see her and find out her status. The next Monday, we met in the designated area for counseling. She looked happy and healthy, and I could see her prison experience had been a good one. She told me how much better it had been for her because there were more opportunities to take advantage of at the prison. It made time pass more quickly.

Over the past three years she had participated in the Kairos retreats, which are the weekend retreats given at the state prisons. She had also become a leader in a Bible study, and attended more advanced computer classes. And she was happy to report her family had come to visit her several times. Knowing her personality, I wasn't surprised to see she didn't allow life to pass her by. In fact, she commented on how hard it was to be back here in the county jail, just sitting and waiting for her day in court.

Before she shared her concerns, she asked me if I would pray with her. We had prayed as a group many times in the past, but this was the first time we had the opportunity to pray one-on-one. She began asking the Lord for strength for the days ahead—the days she would return to the free world. "It's not going to be easy," she said. "My boys are with their father and I won't have much time with them. I need to look for a new job. My mother told me they won't take me back at my former place of employment. I'll need to move in with my mother until I have money to make it on my own." We placed these and her other intentions before the Lord.

After a few weeks, Sharon was released and returned to the trailer home park where her mother resided. I often wonder how she is doing. She hasn't returned to jail—that's a good sign.

Praying with Rosa

Sometimes women are separated from others in the pods. This happens when the crime they are accused of makes them vulnerable to harm by other inmates, or they have shown they cannot live in harmony with a large group. The area designated for these inmates is called lockdown. It serves as a temporary holding place for a few days, or as a long-term residence for several months.

I was asked to meet with Rosa. She was in for the long-term. She had asked Sister if there was any possibility she could be baptized and receive the sacraments. However, she wouldn't be able to leave the lockdown area. Since I was already preparing six other inmates in our group for the sacraments, Sister approached me about adding Rosa to the group. I would need to go to her each week to personally prepare her for these sacraments. Again, I felt God was calling me to minister to this young woman. The following Monday, I received permission to begin meeting with her.

Before we began getting serious about instruction on the sacraments, I wanted to find out more about this young woman. Why was she asking to be brought into the church? What family background might be affecting this decision. She was Hispanic, and her mother was Catholic.

She told me that when she was young, her father (who was not Catholic) would not allow her to be baptized in any religion. And so she grew up experiencing the Catholic faith, but never becoming part of it. In her teenage years, she became pregnant and gave birth to her first child at the age of sixteen. Within seven years, she had four more children, never marrying the father. Abuse came into the family and for reasons—reasons I do not care to know—one of the children died. Both Rosa and her boyfriend are now awaiting trial their involvement with this child's death.

As this young woman of 23 was sitting in the lockdown area, she had lots of time to think. It was during this time she realized she could not go on without the help of God. At one of her visitations with her mother, she asked if it was too late to be baptized. Fortunately, it's never too late for those who want to become part of the Christian community. She put in her request to Sister Ellen, and that's where I came in.

The first time I met with Rosa, she told me about her family, and I could see she was reaching out for help. It is never my intent to find out why any of the women I minister to are serving time. My focus is to help them move forward with their lives—to guide them in their personal faith journey. Sometimes they tell me what crime they have committed, or at least the crime they have been arrested for. I believe they do this when we reach a certain trust level. I do not allow it to affect my relationship with them. Who am I to judge? If it does anything, it makes me more sensitive to their pain.

WILL YOU PRAY WITH ME?

Rosa and I continued to meet weekly for five months. This coincided with the time I was meeting with the larger group to prepare them for their reception of the sacraments. During our sessions, we would talk about what the sacraments mean, and I would leave material for Rosa to read during the week. These papers would give her an opportunity to read and re-read what we had discussed. The following week, I would ask her if she had any questions before we moved on. She told me her mother was so happy she was finally coming into the church, and they often talked about what she was studying.

The day the bishop arrived for the celebration of the sacraments of Eucharist and confirmation, I mentioned we had another candidate, someone who was ready to be baptized, but she was in a special area. I asked him to accompany me through the halls to the lockdown unit after the group celebration was completed. I knew this bishop was very pastoral and would agree to this.

Rosa was ready. Finally, she would officially become part of the church of her childhood. As I watched the bishop pour the water over her, there were tears flowing from her eyes as well. I had never seen her so happy as she was at that moment.

I continued to meet with Rosa for almost a year after that day. In the meantime, her mother has adopted her children and is preparing to have them baptized. Rosa was able to see them for the first time in over a year. When I came to meet her, all she could do was talk about how wonderful it was to see them again. The road ahead is not going to be easy for her. Soon she will be leaving to begin her sentence at the state prison. She tells me she's at peace and will just take each day as it comes. And after all these months of praying with her, I will begin to pray for her.

Along with these requests for prayers from individuals in counseling, there are often pleas for intercession during our weekly meetings. We usually include these petitions in our closing circle of prayer. But I remember one day when we had to actually stop our class midstream and pray.

Julie had told us earlier there was turmoil in her section. She said one of the women told her she had to become hard in order to make it. She had to speak her mind. Julie told us she didn't like that. That wasn't who she was. Now she was feeling bad. She felt like she should not have walked away. A few minutes later, we could hear the loud speaker announcing "Code 2 in 6B." Code 2 meant there was a disturbance in area 6B. This was Julie's section. She broke into tears when she realized they were breaking up a fight in her unit. She looked at me as if to say, "What can we do about this?" Somebody said, "Let's pray." And so we did. We stopped and prayed. Together we asked for God's help for the women in 6B.

Whether individually or as a group, it's comforting to know these women will ask you to join them in prayer. And we know God is listening.

Chapter 11

OTHER OPPORTUNITIES
FOR GROWTH AND
ENRICHMENT

LIFE IS ALL about choices. We are who we are because of the choices we have made in this life. The women serving time will readily admit they haven't always made the right choice. Now they are paying the consequences. They also admit they can change this by beginning to make better choices. And they can begin now.

Every day in jail, they have the option of planning their day. They can decide to lie in their bunks and sleep, sit around and watch television, or play cards. Better yet, they can take the initiative to do something positive, something worthwhile, something that will make them a better person.

Almost all jails and prisons are blessed with hundreds of volunteers, men and women who give their time and talent to help the incarcerated improve their life. The county jail where I volunteer houses more than four thousand men and women. But the good news is there are over three hundred adults who volunteer to offer their support through counseling, classes, and church services. And the inmates need only fill out a green form or sign up to take advantage of these services.

Periodically, all of the volunteers gather for an in-service day, an opportunity to help them in their ministry. I remember the first such day when we met at a large church hall. There were over two hundred men and women, all ages, all denominations, of various ethnic backgrounds. I was impressed. You could feel the power of the Spirit in this assembly. And the more I heard of the numerous different services they were participating in, the more privileged I felt to be part of this community.

Our day began as we gathered in the main hall to unite in prayer and song. A keynote speaker set the tone for the day, providing inspiration for our ministry. After that, we separated into different rooms for the various workshops. These sessions were geared to improve our skills and allow us an opportunity to seek advice. They were truly worthwhile. In fact, I often refer to the notes taken at these gatherings when I get into a problem situation at the jail.

Just as we hope the women in jail will grow from our meetings with them, so we hope to be nourished by these professional gatherings. I recall comments by an elderly woman sitting next to me at the opening session. She said, "I've been helping out at the county jail for almost twenty years now. And I never stop learning new ways to relate to the women. I'm so grateful we have this time to come together, not only to learn more, but to get recharged."

The gathering concludes with a prayer service. During this service we are invited to recommit ourselves to our ministry to the incarcerated. We go forth ready to carry out that commission.

There are so many ways this preparation day reaches into the jail. Ministers go forth ready to share their gifts with the incarcerated women and men. It would be impossible to touch upon all of them in one chapter. However, you'll get an idea of the impact of these volunteers by focusing in on a few of their classes with the women in the main county jail annex.

Since the theme of this book is on the faith journey of women in jail, we'll focus on what is happening in a few classes with a religious emphasis. We have already taken a detailed look at the experiences of the women in the class I lead each week: the sessions where we take the gospel message of the week and apply it to life; the classes where we prepare women to receive other sacraments in the church; and the special gatherings for retreat weekends.

But what about the other meetings that are held for the women's spiritual growth?

Let's begin with the class entitled "Spiritual Growth." For the past seven years, Michelle has met weekly with a group of women, to guide them in their spiritual growth. I was interested in what happened during these weekly sessions. I met with Michelle to find out. And the longer we talked, the more I realized how similar our experiences were with the women. She began by sharing how her own life was enriched through her relationships during these classes.

"I feel these women give back to me more than I ever give to them," she said. Michelle's background in clinical pastoral counseling brought her into this ministry, and she believes her interaction with the women keeps her in touch with this work. She continued, "Even though I have had a few classes with the men, I am really drawn to work with the women. I feel I can relate better to their issues."

And so each week she meets with between ten and twenty woman, to help them pursue their spiritual journey. Her emphasis is on creating a space for them—a space that is nourishing, a space away from the chaos that surrounds them each day. She says:

> "My class is very open-ended, and in many ways the women set the agenda. I want to meet their needs on that day. I guess I am more of a facilitator than a teacher, because my aim is to establish a healthy dialogue. I try to focus my group toward the mystery of human life, and the mystery of God, and how intimately they are connected. Through our brokenness, we come to light and learning. I hope to help the ladies think about their lives in ways that help them to honor their experiences in the light of love, learning, and healing. We always begin with music and prayer followed by a time of quiet, time to set the mood for reflection."

She relayed an experience in her group that occurred a few weeks earlier. It concerned one of the victims of the hurricane Katrina disaster. She said, "Sheila told her story of the event in tears, describing in great detail how she was waiting on the rooftop for help, watching dead bodies float by. She said she had never been able to talk about this before. As she told her story, the others were able to show compassion to her. Her sharing helped her see the sacredness of this experience. And it gave us a sense of reverence in the face of human tragedy."

As I listened to Michelle, I could imagine this group and the dynamics that were occurring as they met. It was obvious these women were reaping the benefits of a woman who cared about them and walked with them in faith. I believe she gives us a model of women ministering to other women.

Besides expressing themselves in dialogue, there are two other classes that offer the women an opportunity to creatively express themselves. One of these is an eight-week spiritual journaling course, and the other a six-week "Art as Prayer" seminar. Both of these sessions are popular with the inmates. Yet each one uses a different medium for expression.

Sister Ellen, one of the chaplains at the jail, conducts the course on spiritual journaling. She herself believes in the positive effects of writing your thoughts daily.

She is passing on to the women all she has learned from taking a similar course. In her introduction, she reminds the women this is not about keeping a diary. It's not a record of what happens each day, but rather, this is like a dialogue—a dialogue with God. In their writings, they should feel free to write each day whatever they want. No one will read this. It is between themselves and God. It is a form of prayer.

Hopefully, these women will carry this practice of journaling back into the free world. It can be one of the positive things they take with them when their sentence is over and they are released. The more positive life skills these women acquire, the more chance they have to make it.

The other seminar offers another vehicle for prayer—praying through art. The course is called Visual Spiritual Journaling—Art as Prayer. And you don't have to be an artist to participate. The goal of this class is to help the participants learn how to incorporate art as prayer into their daily spiritual practices. The following themes were covered over the six week period: What is God saying to me?; My spiritual lifeline; What are my spiritual gifts?; What is my image of God or "The Holy"?; What symbol represents my relationship with God today?; Where is my quiet place of prayer?

Sister Ellen talking to the group

When I met Maripat, the teacher for this group, I asked her if I could join them for one of their weekly classes. She invited me to stay for the current class; it was their sixth and final session. Since some of the students were also in my faith sharing class, I immediately felt at home. In fact, I was delighted when a few of them invited me to join their group at one of the tables.

She began the session by welcoming everyone back, and inviting them to share with the group any thoughts or reflections from the previous week's gathering on symbols and images. As I listened to their comments, I realized a small community had been created over the past six weeks together. The openness and willingness to relay their thoughts and feelings with everyone was obvious. They were ready to share their pain as well as their joys.

Each week, the class officially begins with music and prayer, and a new, prayerful way to create a visual image is introduced. The theme of this week's class is "Finding My Quiet Place of Prayer," finding that place where we can truly feel at peace with ourselves and the universe. While music is playing, we are invited to close our eyes and think of what that place looks like. And when we are ready, we're encouraged to draw that scene. A sense of quiet prevails as the women begin to create their scenes.

After sufficient time has been given for each person to complete a scene, we discuss the scene we have drawn with the others at our table. I remember Sandra telling us, "I always return to the water for peace, for my place of prayer. Here I'm sitting, watching a small river moving slowly along. There are only sounds of birds and the water rippling. I can talk to God as I sit here. There is nothing to disturb me or bother me …at least for this moment."

The others also add their thoughts, scenes of mountain tops, rocking chairs on porches, small chapels, etc. Everyone listens; no one critiqued or commented. This in itself is a moment of prayer.

Journaling in art and in words are two powerful media for the women. However, they are not the only courses for spiritual renewal. Throughout the week, other classes are scheduled for the women, classes on centering prayer, making peace with your past, and women on the way, to mention a few. The reality is that there is no excuse for the women not to take advantage of the numerous opportunities provided to them by the volunteers. The choice is theirs—stay in your pod, or sign up and be counted among those who want to seek God with the help and support of others.

Chapter 12
THE REVOLVING DOOR

LINDA CAME RUSHING into the room, all excited to see me again. She greeted me with a huge smile and the words, "I'm back!" I was really surprised to see her, and, I must confess, a little disappointed. Being back meant something had gone wrong. She really belonged back in the Midwest with her family.

Six months earlier, Linda had been released from the county jail, heading back to Illinois on a Greyhound bus. I remember how anxious she was to return home in time for her eldest son's eighth grade graduation. A few days before she departed, we had talked about her family situation. She said she was so grateful for her mother's generosity in taking care of her four boys while she was incarcerated, and she was happy that now she would be able to take over again. She also shared with me some of the problems she had with her friends and drinking. I promised to keep her and her family in my prayers. It wasn't going to be an easy road.

In fact, her return to the jail showed me it must have been too hard. She confessed she just wasn't ready the last time. "I told them I thought I needed some serious program for rehab. And now I know for sure I need such a program. I can't keep doing this. It's not fair to my mother. It's not fair to my children. I'm working with the system now to get the help I need. They told me I'd be released into a six-week program of rehab. After that, I can return home. Meanwhile, I want to be part of your group again, and hopefully make a retreat."

Linda did stay long enough to make a retreat before beginning her program of rehabilitation. And when it came time to say goodbye again, I believe she was ready. Five years have passed and she hasn't returned.

It's not unusual for inmates to return to jail more than once. In fact, it's so common that jail is often referred to as "the revolving door." I remember asking the group of women in our chapel group how many had been here before. Over half of the hands went up in response. I was curious why this happens so often. And so I asked the women.

They told me there are several reasons women return to jail. It's certainly not because they want to. For many, it's too hard to break the cycle. They return to the same place, the same crowd, and the same crimes. They don't intend to do this. It just happens. I recall Sally saying, "I really wanted to stay clean. But I couldn't keep a job that would pay my rent and all my expenses. Every time an employer found out I had a record, I was dismissed. I had only one alternative for money. And the old gang welcomed me back with open arms. So here I am. This is my third arrest. It's going to be my last one. I just have to be more persistent in following the right path. Now that God is part of my life, I think I can stick to it."

Fortunately, there are companies who are willing to hire women with a criminal record. It's important for the women to be honest when filling out their applications, and state their conviction. One time Sylvia was voicing her concern about getting a job after her release. One of the other women tried to give her hope by saying, "You know, I look at it this way. Since Jesus has forgiven me of my sin, my crime, I can begin anew. And when I'm ready to apply for a job, my slate is clean. So why should I mark down my past criminal record?" The system doesn't work that way. This discussion opened the door for us to talk about the importance of being honest. I hope all the women benefited from this example of what not to do.

While we were discussing job opportunities, Maricella interrupted with her good news. She said, "My boss promised me he'd keep my position open for me. I'll have a job the minute I'm free again." It's great to know that level of trust still exists.

Not everyone is as fortunate as Maricella. There's no one waiting to hire them. And it's tempting to not even try. It's just too discouraging. The lure of easy and fast money looms before them. If they weaken and reconnect with their old gang, it's usually only a matter of time before they are picked up and put back in jail. And the cycle goes on.

One of the other reasons women return to jail is related to being sent out on probation. This period can be anything from a few months to several years, depending on the crime. And because it's not being totally free, it can be broken. If it is violated, they're back. Lilia told me what the terms of probation are. She added, "You feel like someone is always looking over your shoulder, just waiting to catch you if you mess up." She's right. When you are given a period of probation, you are, in truth, still serving time. It's just not at the county jail.

Lilia continued by telling me about her experience, adding why she was now back here in the county jail. "I just got careless about reporting in to my probation officer. Before I knew it, there was an officer at my door, waiting to bring me back to jail. It was a stupid thing to do, and I learned my lesson the hard way."

Veronica chimed in, "I'm back, too, but it wasn't because I didn't report in. I knew how important that was. Unfortunately, I wasn't as good about reporting in for my Narcotics Anonymous group. I knew all the stuff they were trying to tell me. It just seemed like a waste of time. I was wrong. This is the third time I've been arrested, and this is the last time. I guess it just took me longer to get my wake-up call."

I learned from the women that all probations are not the same. Sometimes you are asked to do community service. This can be anything from doing volunteer work at a local church to picking up trash along the highway. Many times there are fees and fines to be paid as well. And as long as you are on probation, you are not truly free.

I was surprised when Hilda told me she had been sent to jail five times already, and it took all this time before she realized her life was missing something important. "I wasn't into my Bible, my church, or anything like that before," she responds. "Yes, I've learned a lot. I was suffering when I came back to jail. This time I asked for a Bible, and it has changed me. I have been walking with God for almost a year now. It's the best thing that has happened to me. Soon I will go to court. This time, God has His hand out. I will take it and not let go."

Whether it's two times or ten, the story seems to be the same. It took those repeated arrests before these women saw a reason to change, and took the opportunity to turn their lives around. For Doreen, it did take ten times, or at least ten arrests. She reports, "I know I was called back to find God and myself. To discover why I was created, and what I was called to become in this life. I wavered from God and fell. But He's holding me in His arms again…I have learned to seek Him and ask Him for help." She continues with advice for others, "Stay with the Lord. Seek Him and ask Him for help. We all slip, but He is always there to pull us up. We must reach out our arms and call His name."

One recurring message seems to be about priorities. Ann reminded me of this when she said, "I was called back to stop, and think about my priorities. I had chosen some of the wrong people to be around. I ended up getting into a fight and was hurt. I could have been killed." For her, returning to jail meant another chance to slow down, to look for God once again.

The Scriptures are filled with stories of compassion and forgiveness for the sinner. They remind us of how God never stops caring for us, no matter how many times we turn away. I believe many women who return to the jail again and again eventually understand this message.

Chapter 13

FROM JAIL TO PRISON

T WAS A beautiful Saturday morning in Texas—a good time to take a leisurely drive through the hill country and into the ranchlands, and we were going to do just that. Sister Teresa and I were on our way to visit Agnes, an inmate we had come to know during her four-year stay at the county jail. Although visits at the state prisons are usually limited to family members, for Agnes it was different. Her family lived overseas, and she wasn't sure they would ever be able to visit her because of the cost of travel. Therefore, we decided we could at least do the second-best thing and visit her as friends. Since both of us had acted as spiritual directors for this young woman over the past four years, we were given a letter of permission to visit.

However, it was not just a matter of driving 100 miles to the prison and asking to see her. This journey actually began several months earlier. First we were asked to present the specific documents verifying our ministerial status and qualifications. After this was approved, we were sent an official letter allowing us an opportunity for visitation at the state prison. The letter did, however, limit our rights for this visit. We were hoping for a contact visit—a chance to be able to sit at a table and talk with our friend. Unfortunately, this is reserved for family members. We would be restricted to meeting with Agnes through a glass screen, using a telephone to communicate. At least we could see her.

As we arrived at the designated unit, we were told that there would be an hour long wait, since it was time for countdown. It was obvious we were novices at this. However, it was definitely worth the wait. Seeing the beautiful smile on her face made the four-hour drive, plus the extra hour wait, priceless. She looked radiant! She was so happy we had come to see her. I can only imagine how difficult it must be for her to watch the other inmates be called out to see their family members week after week—only to be left behind. I remember when I was away at college, how much I looked forward to weekends when my family came to visit, and my disappointment when they couldn't make it. Yet this was nothing compared to what Agnes had endured over the past six months.

As she began to tell us how happy she was we were here, I noticed she looked different than the last time I saw her—the week before she left the county jail. When I commented on this, she immediately responded, "Because I work outside each morning for almost four hours, the sun has darkened my complexion. And doing the manual labor has helped me to lose weight. I have lost almost thirty pounds, and I feel so much better." It was easy to see this environment had been a more positive one than the county jail.

She began by telling us how much she likes her early morning job. "Each morning, we gather at 6:00 A.M. to be driven to the fields in order to start our work by 6:30 A.M. I love watching the sun rise each day. I even forget about all the things that bother me while I'm outside working. For at least at this moment, I am free to see the beauty of nature and the gift of a new day." And as she was telling us about her job, it was clear she really did like it.

We were allowed to stay for two hours with Agnes. According to the regulations, we were able to buy her a drink and snacks while we visited. However, she was so focused on talking to us that she almost forgot to enjoy these treats.

She was anxious to tell us about her recent experience with the chapel community. Since our chapel involvement had brought us together in the first place, she knew we'd be interested in hearing about this. Now at the prison, she was introduced to a new retreat format. It was called *Kairos*. And just two weeks ago, she participated in her first *Kairos* retreat. I could tell by her face it had been a very good faith experience for her. She went on to explain the details of how this retreat was initiated.

She said, "These religious days are offered to the women every few months, and are conducted by the ladies in the local Christian church. They use a lottery system to decide who is chosen to attend. If you are interested in participating in the retreat, you place your name in a bowl. Before they draw out any names, the women pray to the Spirit for guidance in selecting the participants. After they have drawn out the required number of names, they add a few more in order to compile a list of alternates who will take the place of women who change their mind about attending the weekend. My name was one of those on the alternates list. And I was so happy when they contacted me to tell me there would be a place for me on the next retreat."

Because her retreat experiences in the county jail had been so meaningful, she was anxious to participate in a retreat at the prison. She figured it would be different, but the focus would be the same—a time to pause and reflect on your own spiritual journey with the Lord.

We could see she was not disappointed as she shared with us how wonderful these days of prayer and community-building were. In fact, she mentioned that her best friends are now the women in the *Kairos* group. They formed a faith community that has extended beyond their weekend together. Each week, they gather to pray, read, and reflect on Scripture. They also remind each other of the promises they made while on retreat. It motivates them to continue their walk with God. As she told us of the joys of this weekend, her face mirrored that same joy.

Her other news was about her children. Agnes has two young children, a son and a daughter who are being raised by her mother back home. The last time they were together was after her trial—about nine months ago. She doesn't know the next time she will see them, so it's important that she keeps in contact with them in the only way she can—by letters and phone calls. Again, she is at a disadvantage because of the long distance between them. She is allowed to receive a call every 90 days, but for only five minutes. What a contrast to the world where cell phones keep families connected almost every minute. She does try to make up for the lack of phone contact with frequent letters. She told us her daughter just sent her a ten-page letter. She feels her young girl is reaching out to her mother through these letters. So Agnes sent her back a lengthy response. Later, she learned her young son wanted to know why he only got a one-page letter when his sister received so many pages.

She was excited about a reading program where you can read a book to your child, record it on a tape and conclude with a personal message. Since her children only understand books in their native language, she was searching for children's books in foreign languages. She had written me earlier about this program, knowing I had some contacts overseas. Fortunately, I was able to have my cousin in Europe purchase a few books—two for the young boy and a larger anthology for the older girl. I worked with a bookstore to have them sent to Agnes. She received the three books I had sent, and she was able to find more children's books in her native language at the prison. The things we take for granted, such as reading to our children before bedtime and having them near us all the time, must be some of the hardest things these parents endure while serving time in prison.

As the two-hour visit came near an end, Agnes was given notice that she had just a few minutes left. She asked if Sister and I would pray with her before we left. While we each placed our hands against the glass facing each other, tears came to our eyes. God hears us and touches us in the strangest places. It is in giving that we do receive.

About a year later, Sister Teresa and I decided to surprise Agnes with another visit. It had been too long since we had last seen her, even though each of us kept up with her life through regular letter writing.

When she appeared at the window, she was really surprised and happy to see us again. I think she had just about written us off as visitors. Fortunately, others from the ministry had come to see her during the past year. We promised her we wouldn't let so much time pass before we returned for our next visit.

Again, she looked good. She has never been one to complain about her situation, and this shows in her countenance. During our visit, she told us all about her new job. She said, "As much as I liked working outdoors, I had to stop because my arms were covered with rashes. I think it was poison ivy or something like that. Now I help out in the laundry and I really like it. It means starting work at 4:30 in the morning, but I'm finished by 9:30 A.M. and I go back to bed. I need more sleep—three hours at night just isn't enough." We agreed.

She now plays the guitar for the *Kairos* group which meets each Wednesday. It was obvious to us how important this involvement was to her. "I look forward to this weekly meeting. We practice for almost four hours before the group gathers. This gives us time to play, to pray, and to share as well. The large group, usually about fifty or so, joins us in the evening for our prayer service." For Agnes, who is shy by nature, this is an opportunity for her to express herself.

We talked about her upcoming visit with her family. Money collected from a Christian church, plus a loan taken out by the family, is making this possible. She's trying not to get too excited about it, because there are still several uncertainties as to the time, and how many family members will be able to come. At least it is giving her something to look forward to, something to hope for in the midst of the dull routines of prison living.

Before we left, we again joined hands through the glass and prayed together. We prayed for those who are working on her appeal, for Agnes and her family, and for the gift of this time together. We asked God to give this young woman the courage and strength she needs as she spends her days waiting for what the future will bring. We concluded with a blessing, and a promise to return.

Communicating through Letters

Even though we have only visited Agnes twice since her prison term began, we have been able to keep in touch with her through monthly letters. She writes each of us, and we respond in turn. It keeps us in contact when we can't be there with her.

Over the years, many of the other women have written to me while they are serving their sentence at the state prisons. In fact, it's not unusual for me to be writing to at least three women at any given period. Many times, I'll just send them an encouraging card to let them know they are not forgotten. For security reasons, we never give out our home address, so all correspondence is done through our ministry office at the county jail. I always get excited when I see a letter in my mailbox on Monday afternoon, and I look forward to reading it as soon as the class is over.

I've kept all the correspondence from the past ten years, and recently re-read the large folder of letters. If I ever have thoughts of discontinuing this ministry, going over these letters would put an end to that. Since it would be impractical to attempt to share all these individual letters, I will focus in on areas of interest and quote from just a few. You'll get the message.

I'll begin with some positive thoughts these women have written to me. I've received numerous cards from Annette, who I came to know during her stay at the county jail. Her words have always been filled with gratitude and hope. On one occasion she wrote:

"God is working very strongly in my life … There are a lot of great people that come here to minister to us in this unit, just as you did in the jail. I have had the honor of hearing some wonderful and moving testimonies in our church services. For a maximum security prison, this place has a lot to offer. That to me is such a God thing, it is hard to put down on paper. I am free in prison. Who would have thought that was possible? Certainly not me. That is God and only God at work … And as I awake each day here, I am seeing the beauty that He wants me to see. Yes, it can be ugly if I choose to look at it through negative eyes, but by God's grace, I choose not to … When I arrived here I wasn't so lonely because you and all the other ladies had prepared me. You had given me a solid foundation for my faith. For that, I will be forever grateful. And I will do my best to share it with those God puts into my life ..."

Later on, in one of her cards, Annette tells how she ministers to others. "I'm doing what I can to help the new women to adjust here. When we can't talk, I just send them a smile of encouragement. I think sometimes that smile says more than words." It's encouraging to see how the chain of giving goes on.

Church is important for Nancy, too. She lets us know she's doing all right in the midst of prison life. "I'm doing OK," she writes. "Prison isn't that bad when you have the Lord on your side. I'm in one of the smaller units, so it's a little easier, but the place isn't any better because it's still prison. Church here is great! We have all kind of ministries come visit us. And I'm also in the choir, so I get to sing praises, just like I did in the county jail."

There are other words to uplift our spirits, as Judy writes, "Yesterday it was raining outside, and everyone seemed to be in a hurry, as if they would melt. Not me, though. I took my time. It has been almost two years since I have been able to feel its moisture on my skin. It is truly a blessing how the Lord waters over his earth for us. It is the simplest things in life that now bring me joy ..."

Julie makes a similar comment in her letter. "I have been trying my very best to be as positive as possible. I read my Bible continuously. Also, we are able to walk outside to the chow hall, so I am able to see the flowers, trees, birds, and the sky."

But all is not sun and flowers. The climate is different on the inside. Stella comments, "I really, really, really hate it here. I have never seen so many mean and rude women in all my life. It's a battle I go through every day, being called names or threatened ... I don't know how much longer I can humble myself. But every time I want to lash out or fight, I think of my kids and humble myself. Lately, it is really hard."

Debra reminds us that prison isn't the same as jail, as she relays, "It is a whole different world in here. I am still in major shock ... I came here expecting to have a lot of spiritual groups like we had in the jail. But instead, I have to fight and claw my way to the door with thirty-five other women to get the few available seats for church. It blows my mind! I study by myself. I wish anything to be back in our group … I know I can change this situation into triumph. I just have to keep God in sight."

Good things do happen, even in bad situations. Shirley will attest to that, as she tells us, "Now I have some blessings to share with you. My long overdue prayers are being answered. I have finally found peace … As you know, my faith really took a leap backward when I left the county, and I've been struggling to get back ever since. Well, now I am back. I've learned to trust God for everything. But most of all, I've learned not to dwell on my past failures. I can finally forgive myself."

Shirley continued to write me during her entire time at the state prison. And since she has returned home, she has written me at the detention center to inform me she is reunited with her family and continues to feel at peace.

Over and over, I get the message of how important it is for these women to get cards and letters from both family and friends. I think of it as the ministry of the printed word. It's one way we can minister to those who are separated from us by the walls of the prison.

A Christian Prison

Somehow, this seems like a misnomer … the words "prison" and "Christian" in the same title. But it is actually a very real institution, and I had the good fortune to be able to meet with someone who was assigned to this special minimum security unit.

I first became aware of the program called *Inner Change* through a friend who lived near Sugarland, Texas, where it began. Cal had become a mentor to an inmate, and was aware of the power of befriending the incarcerated. When he offered to bring me to this prison to learn more about the program, I couldn't refuse. It was an eye-opener for me. Good things do happen in the strangest places.

I met the chaplain, Jerry Brian, at the entrance, and we proceeded to a large meeting room where we sat and talked. He did most of the talking as I questioned him about this unique approach to working with the incarcerated. During the following hour and a half, I decided to take notes so as not to forget the details of life here.

He told me that one had to volunteer to be placed here, and because their space was limited, volunteers had to be screened. This was not a place for everyone. The strict regimen and religious environment would only appeal to a few. But for those who chose it, it could transform an entire life.

We talked about a typical day. The inmates are awakened in time to attend the 5:00 A.M. morning prayer. After breakfast, they work at their assigned jobs until lunch time. In the afternoon, classes are held in Christian living, Bible studies, and life skills, as well as high school equivalency courses. There's no time for sleeping in the pods, playing cards, or watching television during the day. In the evening, they will again gather for seminars, guest speakers, more Christian teaching, and worship services. By 10:00 P.M., all presentations are over. Since morning rising comes early, most are in bed as soon as possible.

I couldn't help but think of how much this routine sounded like the schedule of a seminary, monastery, or convent. These inmates are guided to let their faith permeate their whole day, their whole week, very much as all Christians are reminded to not limit their faith to a Sunday ritual but live the message of the gospel.

Jerry also explained how the community outside is included in this program. After six months in the program, each inmate is given a mentor from one of the local churches. This person not only connects to the inmate while serving time, but continues to walk in faith with them for at least six months following their release.

When I asked him how this all started, I was told it opened in 1997 and was operated by Prison Fellowship. I remembered reading of the work of Charles Colson, the man who served time for his involvement with the Watergate scandal. This was one more fruit of his effort to change things within prisons, to help those incarcerated break the cycle of crime. It was during his own imprisonment that Charles Colson had seen and experienced the difference that faith in Jesus Christ makes in the lives of people. He became convinced that the real solution to crime is found through spiritual renewal. When he founded Prison Fellowship, he had no idea how many lives it would touch. This Christian prison unit is just one example of its outreach.

Does this Christian focus truly make a difference? It will take years to give us the statistics on the recidivism rate of those who participate in this program, however everyone is optimistic this environment will make a difference. But more than statistics is the realization that lives are dramatically changed. God, not crime, has become the focal point for these men.

Chapter 14

THE FIRST STEPS TO A BETTER LIFE

THE CLOCK READS 3:45 P.M. on a Monday afternoon. It's time to leave the jail after my weekly session. I enter the reception area, filled with adults waiting to visit their loved ones who are incarcerated, and I notice a familiar face in the crowd. The young African-American woman recognizes me as well, and calls me by name. I respond with a smile and walk over to talk to her.

"Gail," she says, "It's so good to see you. Do you remember me?" Unfortunately, I have never been good at recalling names. So in order to avoid embarrassment I respond, "You look so familiar. I know we must have met somewhere." She answered with a smile, "Yes, we did meet, and it was right here at the jail. My name is Olivia, and I was part of the group making the weekend retreat in 1999. You were the leader at our table. I'll never forget that weekend. I even remember the theme—The Lord is My Shepherd. And He was my shepherd during those three days. What a wonderful experience that was for me. It really was the point I began to change my priorities."

Wow! Here it was, eight years later, and someone was standing before me in the jail annex waiting room, clutching her Bible and telling me about a key moment in her life. Here was living proof that life can get better.

She continued, "Remember what I told you on that last day of the retreat?" So far, I was not doing well when it came to remembering anything—her name, the time we first met, the theme of the retreat, to say nothing about a conversation that took place. But I was anxious to hear what she was going to tell me, so I let her continue.

"At that time," she said, "I was really into drugs big time. I didn't like myself and I wanted to begin to change my ways. The love and testimonies of the women on that weekend opened that door for me. I felt called to be a part of something like this, called to share my faith the way they were doing. They were all so happy and in love with the Lord. After the last presentation, I said to you, 'When I get out of here and I'm clean again, I'm going to find out what it takes to become a minister in my church.' And I did just that. I went to school and took all the necessary steps to prepare for my role in the church—to spread the Good News among the needy. Over the past three years, I've been going to one of the state prisons and now I come here—to my old pods. I bring my Bible, and we read Scripture and pray together."

Meeting Olivia that afternoon really made my day. Here is a person who can say, "I know what it's like because I've been there, done that." I could tell she was happy to be able to share her stories of ministry, and how she had followed through on her retreat resolution, and I was happy for her.

Before we parted, she wanted to tell me a little about her work at the state prisons. She said, "I really like working with the men who think they are tough and don't need anyone, especially God, in their life. I tell these guys, 'Listen, I know where you're at. I was there too. I did drugs 'cause I thought that was important in life. But then I woke up. I realize that being right with God is what it's all about. And before you ruin yourself, your family, and your future, you'd better change. You can do it if you try. I did. It's not easy—I can tell you that for a fact—but it's worth the price. And I promise I'll pray with you and for you, so it can happen."

Olivia has walked in their shoes. What a great testimony for the women and men she encounters. I admire her zeal and enthusiasm, and pray there are many others who follow in her footsteps.

It Happened at Denny's

It was a Thursday evening and my husband and I had just enjoyed a good basketball game at the nearby Alamodome. All the restaurants in the area were busy with the after-game crowd, and since we weren't that hungry, we decided to pop into the Denny's restaurant for a quick bowl of soup before returning home.

When the waitress approached our table to take our order, she kept looking at me, staring at me as if she recognized me. Finally she said, "You look familiar. I'm trying to place where we've met before."

This happens to me quite often because of my involvement in parish work, and my role as a presenter at workshops, so I was not taken aback. I began listing the different parishes I worked in, as well as talks I had recently given. But none of these struck a cord with her. And then she remembered. "I know where we met. It was at Bexar County (meaning the detention center). I was in your church group. In fact, I was in it just a few months ago, before I was released." What a great moment of reuniting. How good it was to see one of the women adjusting back to a normal life. Her face beamed as she proudly told me of her present status. She said she continues to go to church, and now brings her three children. This job is helping pay her rent, and she feels she is getting back on her feet.

It just happened to be two weeks before Christmas—a perfect excuse for giving her a generous tip. As we parted, I gave her a warm embrace and dropped some extra cash in her pocket, telling her to buy something for her children. Her Christmas gift to me was the happiness she has found. I'm so glad those other restaurants were too crowded that night.

Letters from Home

Once inmates are released from the county jail and return home, it usually means there will be no opportunity to continue the connection made while they were serving time. Jail regulations prohibit us from exchanging addresses. However, if one of the women wants to write us, they are able to do so through the detention ministry address—that is the county jail address. Every so often I get a letter or card from one of the women, telling me about their present circumstances and what it's like to be free again.

One Christmas, I received season's greetings from Sharon, with pictures of her children and a warm hand-written message, "You are always in my heart and prayers. I'm doing great! So busy that time just flies by. I've been working full-time for about a year now. In fact, I even have a car since last December. Here's a picture of my boys. I've been able to be back with them …" Those few words brought back to mind a young woman who was determined to do it right this time. I'd say she's off to a good start.

Another letter I received also filled me with happiness, reading of Sandy's successful transition to the free world. She writes, "I just want to thank you for all your love, kindness, and patience you had shown me during my long stay in jail. I've been out almost five months now, and am doing very well. I'm finishing up my first semester at San Antonio College and getting ready to register for next semester…When I got out of jail, I had the pleasure of teaching my children the song, 'God's Grace Changes Everything,' and they love to sing it around the house. Each time they do, it fills me with warm memories of your loving support." I must admit I think of Sandy and her two children when we sing that song at the jail. She is a testimony to the fact that God's grace does change everything.

I've often thought how good it would be to hear from all the women as they move from jail to home again. But that's impossible. However, just getting that occasional note of "Thanks, and I'm doing fine" is all it takes to keep me on this journey with the women. Multiply these two testimonies by the countless unwritten ones, and we know life can get better.

The Family Renewal Center

All across the country, there are organizations created to help men and women after their release from jail or prison. Even though there never seems to be enough of these centers, the fact that there are some gives us hope there will eventually be more. In our city, we are blessed with the Family Renewal Center. Its goal is to help the formerly incarcerated build new lives, and assist their families in the process. They realize that starting over is not easy, but there is life after incarceration.

One of the major benefits of this center is they provide services for the entire family of the inmates. Since a portion of their staff is formerly incarcerated women, they understand the needs of these women. They've been in their shoes, and so they are able to help the women who come to their office seeking help to find a job. They are at their service, ready to listen and help them in any way they can. If they want to continue in a twelve-step program, one they had begun while serving time, they are guided to the right place. Whatever their needs—a place to study Scripture, help in further counseling, guidance to re-enter a local church—the center is there to help.

A new program is now being initiated from this center to help the families of the incarcerated. It is called *We Are Not Alone* (W.A.N.A.). One of the good things about this program is the fact it will give members of local parishes the opportunity to interact with these hurting families. There will be gatherings at different locations throughout the city where meals will be served, babysitting provided, and support meetings conducted. What a great project for helping families find ways to cope with the stress of arrest, imprisonment and release. And what a good opportunity for adults to volunteer, adults who want to help the incarcerated, but are not comfortable in the jail surroundings.

There are similar programs of support all over the country. All with one purpose—to provide a support system for the women who really do want to take the first steps to a better life.

Chapter 15

. . . .

A HOME AWAY
FROM HOME

I NEEDED A PLACE to return to after I was released from jail. I was searching for a home away from my old home. Away from the people, places, and things that led me astray. Someone told me about such a place. It was called 'Woman at the Well House.' And so I applied and was accepted," said Joanne.

This same story is repeated over and over all across the country. And even though there are places created to answer this need, they are few and far between. The hope is that more such homes will become plentiful: homes created and directed by adults who care about the future of women offenders who want to make a better life for themselves. They are ready to turn their life around, but they need a place to make that happen.

In 1995, a Methodist clergywoman, Georgia Stone, recognized this need when she founded Woman at the Well House in San Antonio, Texas. It was an outgrowth of her prison ministry. She invited church leaders in the area to help her in this endeavor. Together, they were able to provide a home for the homeless and friendless being released from jail.

The scriptural story of the woman at the well tells of the woman rejected by others. This provides the setting for the incarcerated women rejected by society today.

Jesus, tired from his journey, sat down there at the well. It was about noon. A woman from Samaria came to draw water. Jesus said to her, "Give me a drink." The Samaritan woman said to him, "How can you, a Jew, ask me, a Samaritan woman, for a drink?" Jesus answered and said to her, "If you know the gift of God and who is saying to you "Give me a drink," you would have asked him and he would have given you living water." The woman said to him, "Sir, you do not even have a bucket and the cistern is deep. Where then can you get this living water? Are you greater than our father Jacob, who gave us this cistern and drank from it himself with his children and his flocks?" Jesus answered and said to her: "Everyone who drinks this water will be thirsty again; but whoever drinks the water I shall give will never thirst; the water I shall give will become in him a spring of water welling up to eternal life." The woman said to him, "Sir, give me this water, so that I may not be thirsty and have to keep coming here to draw water."

—John 4:6-16

The conversation between Jesus and the woman continues, where he reveals to her all of her past life. She is moved by his words, and is stopped in her conversation with the return of the disciples. They were surprised he was speaking to a woman, but they did not question him.

The woman left her water jar and went into the town and said to the people, "Come see a man who told me everything I have done. Could he possibly be the Messiah?" They went out from town and came to him.

—John 4:28-31

The women coming to live at this house, named after this biblical story, can relate to the woman at the well. They, too, are alienated from society, feeling as though no one wants to associate with them. And just as the woman was given hope by the Lord, so these women are searching for hope and encouragement. And with God's grace, they too will be able to leave, ready to proclaim the good news.

This has, in fact, been shown to happen from the numerous letters and stories written by the residents who have returned to society after spending time at Woman at the Well House. *Wellsprings,* their quarterly publication, has printed many such stories. Here are some worth repeating.

After Debbie was released from prison, she realized she needed to work on herself before returning to be a mom for her young son and two daughters. Someone had told her about Woman at the Well House, and so she appeared at their door. "What has helped me so much there is the sense of family I never had—plenty of 'tough love' mothering, and a sisterhood with the other women residents." In and out of foster and group care since age 10, it gave her a home she never had before. And now her life is taking a new direction. She's starting college classes and planning to eventually work with teens who have drug and alcohol problems, problems she has had to work through in her own life. "I'm learning to accept criticism. I'm exploring my spirituality. I'm learning new tools to help me pull through the tough times. And I'm taking responsibility for my past." That past is over, and Debbie is focusing on keeping her footing in the here and now.

And there is Dee, who keeps giving back to the place that helped her when in need. "When I graduated from the Well House, I made a commitment to give back as freely as I was given to when I was here." She stops into the house almost every week. Sometimes she has her arms full of items the house needs, other times she offers to help with tasks around the place, and then there are times just spent talking to the women who need encouragement. She's been there. And she's ready to listen.

Giving back is a way for Dee to remember how far she has come. Her commitment doesn't end with her work at the Well House. She is also active in a local twelve-step fellowship, as well as going back into the prisons to bring a message of hope and support to others. Like the woman with Jesus, she has a message to bring others.

I was personally drawn to the work at the Well House from its beginning in 1995. However, my involvement was limited to bringing clothes, bedding, books, and paper products to help the ladies. That all changed in summer of 2006, when I was invited to meet with the women for a series of scripture-sharing sessions. At last, I would have the opportunity to get to know the women, a chance to learn what was behind their smiling faces that greeted me with appreciation as we carried in the monthly donations.

Our meetings were scheduled for six consecutive Thursday evenings. We would gather in the living room around 6:30 P.M. to get acquainted. After a few weeks, this became our time to share stories of their past week. At 7:00 P.M., our formal session began with music to set the atmosphere for prayer and reflection. One of the women was invited to lead us in an opening prayer before reading the Scripture passage. My goal was to gradually guide the women to take responsibility for each part of the service, from the opening prayer to the closing hymn, providing them with the tools needed to conduct their own faith-sharing experience.

After the song and prayer, we were ready to spend the next hour making these words from Scripture our own, taking time to look at how they applied to our life at this time, on this day. The Word of God came alive!

One particular evening, we based our reflection and sharing on the story of the Transfiguration of Jesus, taken from the gospel of Mark 9:2-9 which reads:

> After six days Jesus took Peter, James and John and led them up a high mountain apart by themselves. And he was transfigured before them, and his clothes became dazzling white, such as no fuller on earth could bleach them. The Elijah appeared to them along with Moses, and they were conversing with Jesus. Then Peter said to Jesus in reply, "Rabbi it is good that we are here! Let us make three tents; one for you, one for Moses and one for Elijah." He hardly knew what to say, they were so terrified. Then a cloud came, casting a shadow over them; then from the cloud came a voice: "This is my beloved Son. Listen to him." Suddenly, looking around. they no longer saw anyone but Jesus alone with them.

What a powerful gospel reading. The women needed time to think about this message. As I re-read it, I asked them to select a phrase or word that spoke to them, something that touched their mind and hearts.

Since there were only ten of us this particular evening, everyone would have time to share their thoughts. Susan began with the concept of Jesus going off alone, getting away from the noise and confusion of the large crowds. She said, "I'm finding this is important for me. I need to allow time to just be alone, to connect with myself and to connect with my God. That's one of the reasons I came to the Well House…to take time apart from my usual day for quiet, for God."

Madeline added, "This idea of transfigured to me says change. Just as Jesus changed before their eyes, I, too, can change before the eyes of God and others. It also tells me that I need moments of transfiguration just as the apostles did, moments to give me strength to handle the hard times. Jesus knew there would be hard times ahead for his followers and so he gave them this experience. I think He understands my hard times too, and sometimes gives me little glimpses of transfiguration."

And Laurie shared a personal experience from just a couple days ago that she felt fit this gospel. "I met a woman earlier this week whom I had served time with in the state prison. At that time she had been weighed down with her drug addiction. But when I saw her this week she just glowed with happiness. I couldn't believe the change in her. She told me how she had a new job and all that had happened since she returned home. And it gave me hope. I left her feeling changed."

While the other women added their comments, you could feel the presence of the Spirit amongst us. I believe that evening was a "transfiguration" for all of us. In fact, one of the ladies said, "This is so good. I feel like Peter and want to say, 'Let's not leave this spot. Let's build our own tent."

As our summer session came to its end, we had to face the reality of separation. It had been such a positive experience, both for me as well as this group of women. The women were now comfortable opening the service, reading the Scriptures, and to some extent, facilitating the discussion. I planned to leave them handouts covering the next several weeks' gospel readings to help them when they would gather on their own. Now it would be up to them and the work of the Spirit.

During our final evening together, we had a short ceremony. Each woman received a certificate of attendance. I also took this opportunity to get some feedback on the summer series. There was no doubt that this had been a positive experience, but I really wanted to know more about their general comments on living at the Well. Since I was also meeting each week with women at the jail, it would be good to have something concrete to tell them about one of their options for reentry into society.

I began by asking them the basic question concerning their admission to the Well House. "Why did you apply for a place at Woman at the Well House?"

"I wanted to be in an environment so that I wouldn't have to go straight back around those old people, places, and things," replied Becky. And Sarah agreed with her, adding, "I also needed a new place to regroup, a place to get back on my feet, one that reinforced my need for security." Sue, like so many others, had no place to return to. She decided to search for a transitional home that would offer a faith-based structure. She found that at the Well House. In fact, religion was a key factor for many who applied at the Woman at the Well House. Maureen said, "I needed to continue my walk with God outside prison. Here was a place that would make this happen."

This was the home away from home these women were seeking. They were happy they had found it. This became apparent when I inquired what they liked best about being here.

The key word in all their responses was "support." Isabel tells us, "All the women here are supportive. We have a common ground. We are striving for a new way of life." Lynn adds, "The support system is not just from the other residents, but it's also from the staff and those who come to minister to us while we are here." This has helped Maureen, who says she was overwhelmed when she first arrived, but now because of others is a lot calmer and focused. Sue gave the house her strong endorsement. "It works," she said, "I'm

safe, secure, and provided for while I'm putting my life together."
And isn't that why the house was established years ago?

Of course being in a transitional house isn't always easy. I was
interested in what aspects of living here the women found hard. It
appeared the overcrowded schedule was their biggest challenge.
During the years they were incarcerated either at the county jail
or state prison, they had lots of time to just relax. In fact, they
probably had too much time, and it was easy to form bad habits
about the efficient use of one's time. Now they are placed in an
environment where just about every hour is accounted for, and it's
tough. In many ways they are still not free—free to schedule their
own day, go as they wish, or even leave the premises at will. But the
structure of this home has a purpose which leads to a goal—their
independence. By the time they are ready to leave, each woman
must have a job, a bank account with savings, a place to live, and a
church affiliation. This needs to happen in the six months allowed
each resident. And it can happen the way the structure is set up.
During this time, they are asked to adhere to a strict schedule and
follow all the directives. But when they do graduate from the Well
House, there is much celebration and rejoicing.

I was curious about how these women looked to their future.
I was happy to hear how important it was for them to have goals.
Maureen shared with us her plans to get a job and go to college
and major in theology. She added, "While I'm about doing all that,
I plan to stay clean and sober, and raise my girls properly."

Mothering was important to Isabel, too. After this positive
experience, Isabel realized how important good friends are. She
said, "I want to build a network of Christian friends. I also would
like to be self-supporting so I could have my own car and maybe
even a condo." I encouraged her, as well as the others, to hold
fast to their dreams, to write them down, pray about them, and
do something to make them a reality. I told them these were not
impossible dreams, and promised my prayerful support as they
re-entered society.

Over the years, hundreds of women have come and gone from
the Well House. Some weren't able to adjust to the rules and had

to be dismissed, but fortunately they were few in number. Many more have become integrated into society and have made that entry because of the help received during this transitional period.

Recently I came across a couple letters I had received from two of the women who I originally met in the county jail, and later had the opportunity to see at the Woman at the Well House. They both wanted to send words of appreciation to the staff at the Well House, as well as the members of the Board.

Susanne began, "How can I ever begin to thank you for the opportunity of a lifetime? Well House gave me such an incredible advantage; it gave me time to get myself grounded. I came to you at the beginning of January, having just spent four years in prison. I was scared and totally in culture shock, as coming out of incarceration takes some getting used to … Living at the Well House gave me time and support as I was able to get funding, went through training to make myself more marketable, and then found a good job. The timing was not my own; it was God's … I am blessed in so many ways."

In the same theme of appreciation, Cynthia wrote, "I just would like to express my sincere gratitude for all the support and help that Well House has given me over the year that I lived there." She continues:

> "Through the guidance and patience that was so freely given to me I was able to see my world and the world around me in a different light. I do not feel like the same person who walked in the door straight out of prison. I have a wonderful relationship with my parents when there was none before. I have my children at my side and I have a wonderful job that I enjoy immensely, and most important of all … I am a month away from a year of honest sobriety … Well House has given me so much, I will carry it with me for the rest of my life. It is truly amazing how so much of a change takes place when you live at Well House. I would not be where I am today if I would have fought the miracle."

I believe that says it all. The woman at the well was alone, but she left that place ready to proclaim the good news. Today, this story is reenacted by a new woman at the well.

Chapter 16

WHERE DO YOU FIT IN THIS PICTURE?

OVER THE PAST ten years, jail ministry has been a very important part of my life. Besides meeting with the women each Monday afternoon, I've tried to participate in their semi-annual retreats. And it was during both of these times I gathered the material for this book. As mentioned in the opening chapter, this is only one glimpse into what happens behind jail walls. I realize everything that goes on in this setting is not positive: the fights in the pods, the disagreements with the officers, the backbiting and pettiness between inmates. That is also the real world. But I chose to focus on the good things that happen in a strange setting—the county jail. My personal experience has deepened my own faith life, and I hope by sharing it with you, it has also affected your faith. In fact, one of my goals in writing of my experiences with these women was to spark an interest in others to step forward and get involved in this ministry.

That's where you fit in the picture. Your response might echo mine when the pastor invited us to get on the bus. "It's not for me." But before you give your answer, remember that the corporal works of mercy—feeding the hungry and clothing the naked–also include visiting the imprisoned. This should not be ignored. There are many ways to respond to this invitation.

No matter where you live, there is either a local jail or state prison in the vicinity, very much as in the community where I have been involved. Housed within those walls are numerous men and women serving sentences for various crimes. As Christians, the gospel calls us to go forth and spread the good news. And this extends to everyone—even those serving time for criminal offenses. Thanks to in the invitation of Sister Teresa I have been able to minister in this community. She continues to reach out for more workers in the vineyard. Sister, as chaplain of the jail, knows the need for volunteers to help spread God's Word.

Sr. Teresa asking someone to join in this ministry

You may feel unprepared to volunteer to lead a group of women or men. This is often true for laity in the church. For so many years, we have relied on the clergy, religious men and women, and chaplains to minister to the needy. But the times have changed, and it's time for all members of the Christian community to realize the importance of their baptismal call, their call to serve.

WHERE DO YOU FIT IN THIS PICTURE?

Today, there is no excuse for being unprepared. Opportunities for growth and enrichment abound. Just check out the colleges and institutions of learning in your local community. There are numerous courses and classes being offered to prepare men and women for ministry. In fact, many of these classes can be taken online, at home, at your convenience. Courses in scripture and theology will update our knowledge. Courses in group dynamics, counseling, and psychology will provide the skills that help us work with others. We need to take advantage of these opportunities. They will not only enrich our personal spiritual life, but also help us in our ministry.

You can also get practical hands-on training and professional guidance through your area's detention ministry program. You don't need to have a professional degree in teaching or counseling to minister to others. There are certain qualities, however, that are important when considering the call to jail ministry.

When I worked in the catechetical world, I would often have the teachers list qualities they thought were needed to be successful. If I made a similar list for those who are interested in volunteering to do jail ministry, it would include the following attributes:

A faith filled person: It's faith that draws us into this ministry, and it's faith which sustains us in it over time. We often hear, "You cannot give what you don't have," and this applies here, too. We cannot share faith unless we ourselves are faith-filled. Faith is a gift, but it is a gift that grows through our personal prayer life, and a gift that needs to be shared with others.

A good listener: The women and men who are incarcerated are living without their family and friends. They have no one close to talk to, to share their concerns, their feelings, their anxieties. This is where we as facilitators or counselors can be of great help. We need to give them an outlet to vent their feelings. If there is trust built up between us, we can be that person who is missing from their life, at least for this short period.

A non-judgmental person: It's so easy to sit in judgment, to look down on those whom society has named a criminal. However, the gospel reminds us, "Judge not, and you shall not be judged"

(Luke:6:37). The longer I work with the women in jail, the more I see how fragile they are. Many of them have been victims of abuse, of poverty, and other misfortunes. If there is one thing I can do in my ministry, it is to treat each person with dignity, the dignity they deserve as a child of God. It's never my concern why the women are serving time. It is my concern that they are reminded they are good.

A person with a commitment: I've often noticed that, after a parish group has conducted a weekend retreat, one or two of the ladies want to become more involved in the program. However, they never take the time to go through the process of completing the necessary paperwork and getting their own badge. If you really want to become involved in this ministry, there has to be a definite commitment made. Not everyone can offer their services for an ongoing period. For some, it's easier to sign up for a short term, a limited amount of weeks, such as the six-week journaling course. Even more popular are the groups who volunteer for the semi-annual retreats. But whatever commitment you make, take it seriously.

I remember one Monday I had just returned from a long trip. I felt very tired and was tempted to just call in and cancel my weekly session. But then I changed my mind. I just didn't think it was fair to the women.

As the women were arriving for class, Allyson came to the front of the room and with a big smile said, "I've been waiting all morning for this class. When it's Monday I always feel good when I wake up because I know we are going to gather in a few hours to share and pray." As I listened to her and watched her smile, I wondered how I could have even thought of canceling our session, and I was happy I was there.

I'm sure there are other qualities that lend themselves to this ministry: an open mind, a sense of humor, and a caring spirit, just to name a few. As I travel around the country giving talks to Leaders of Faith Formation and teachers, I like to share stories of my ministry at the jail. More than once I have been approached afterward by someone contemplating going into this work. I pray they'll follow this call. I like to remind these groups that the thirty years I worked in parish ministry were a perfect preparation for my ministry in the jail. In fact, many of the jobs people are already doing can prepare them for this work. Teaching religion, facilitating scripture study groups, counseling teens and young adults, ministering to the infirm, and so many other vocations will provide the tools that transfer easily into working with incarcerated men and women.

A Few Differences

Although there are many similarities in spreading the good news, there are also circumstances unique to the jail environment. But these should not stand as a barrier to us in making a commitment. If we are willing to take the leap of faith, take the risk, and step into the unknown, we are on the right course. It's not unusual to fear the unknown, and for most of us, jails and prisons are places we've never experienced.

One particular evening I was meeting with a parish team of volunteers, praying before an upcoming retreat. One of the youngest members of the group, Carolyn, a woman in her mid-twenties, admitted she was scared of the weekend at the jail. She had done several retreats at various parishes, but this was different. The very thought of going inside a jail and staying there all day made her nervous. But she was determined not to let that stop her. She felt God wanted her to have this experience. By the end of the weekend, she was so moved by what she had been a part of she wanted to remain in contact with a couple of the women. They were her age, and related to her during the discussions of the weekend. She told them she could write them through the parish office, as no one is allowed to give a home address. Three lives changed because Carolyn walked in faith and not fear.

It's important to keep in mind it's a privilege to be allowed to enter into these guarded areas. In reality, we are guests of the institution. As guests, we must be aware of the common courtesies that are expected of us. Being friendly to those who are employed in the jail should be a priority. We come for a brief period and are soon gone. These adults spend endless hours taking care of the numerous needs of the women in the units. When they are ready to take the women back to their pods, it's important we cooperate and not cause delays by keeping one of the women back to talk or pray with. There is a time for this, and it's not at the end of our session. It's interesting to see how sensitive the inmates are to those in charge. In fact, it's not unusual for one of the women to add the name of the officer in the room when we are closing with our circle of prayer. I don't think that goes unnoticed.

Before beginning your ministry to the incarcerated, there will be a period of preparation. You will learn the rules and regulations of the particular facility where you will be working. If you are given a handbook, take time to familiarize yourself with it. Keep it handy to refer to when you have questions. You don't want to jeopardize your ministry by breaking any of the regulations.

So much of what you will be dealing with falls under the category of common sense. Common sense is especially called for in the way we dress, as well as the jewelry and makeup we use. There is often a dress code stated in the manual. But if it isn't spelled out, a good guideline to follow is to wear clothes appropriate for attending a meeting or church function, such as a dress, a pants outfit, or good slacks. Jeans, shorts, and sleeveless or low-cut tops certainly don't fall in that category, and fine jewelry and excessive makeup is also inappropriate. Over the past years, I've seen these guidelines violated. It's so important to be sensitive to the group we are ministering to. These women must get tired of wearing the basic blue cotton outfits they are given, even though I never hear complaints about them. When I happen to appear in something blue, they usually tease me about becoming one of them.

It's not uncommon to form healthy friendships when some of the women spend months waiting for their trail. Those who have no family close at hand will turn to you for someone to talk to, and being a good listener is important. However, we must be cautious that we do not become someone they dump all their criticisms on. Being an arbitrator in the system is not your role. No institution is without faults, and the jail is no exception. When someone begins to tell me their complaints, I quickly stop them and let them know they're telling the wrong person. This is one time I can respond, "I don't work here; I'm just a volunteer." Then I encourage them to go to the proper authorities with their grievances.

Even though the situation of ministering in a jail is different from other church ministries, it's not that difficult. And it definitely shouldn't keep us from responding to the call if our hearts are drawn to help these women temporarily separated from us.

Other Options

After considering all the ways you can help in your county jail, you may still respond, "It's not for me." This is true; it isn't for everyone. One woman told me she was in a jail visiting an inmate and heard those iron doors close. She said, "I have this fear of being shut in. I could never do what you're doing, but I would like to help. Is there any way I can still support this cause without going inside the jail?"

Yes, there are other ways to show your support for this group. First, you may have to do some research to find out what is needed in your particular area. Often you can begin by checking with your local church community. I have noticed articles in parish bulletins around the country that refer to either jail ministry or prison ministry groups. These men and women focus on helping the inmates of these institutions, and know their needs. Sometimes they have collections to help their families, especially during the holiday season. Other times they need materials or finances for retreats. They are seeking help from the community at large, and that's where you can show your support.

In some cities, there are houses designated to help those released from jail make the transition to freedom. Since these are usually sponsored by the church and other civic organizations, they also depend on the rest of the community for support, both with finances and volunteer help. There are also centers established to help women and men released from jail make their reentry into society. These centers are another place you can offer to help. In other words, there are many ways you can help which are outside the confines of the jail. Don't let your fear of iron bars and closed doors close your heart to the needs of this community.

And finally, all of us can pray for the countless women and men who are serving time. I mentioned that we close every class with our circle of prayer. During this time, each person mentions someone or something she would like all of us to pray for. I have often brought my personal needs before this group. As we pray for them and their needs, they are praying for us and our needs.

Over the years, hundreds of women have joined our group for prayer and song, for sharing and caring. I've often commented on the fact that I hoped we would meet again, but not under these circumstances. And then I would add, "If not in this life, let's all have a great celebration in the next." I truly believe we are all seeking God while serving time—our time on earth.

Printed in the United States
218462BV00001B/2/P

9 781414 111643